God's Revolution

The Witness of Eberhard Arnold

edited by the
Hutterian Society of Brothers
and
John Howard Yoder

preface by
Malcolm Muggeridge

PAULIST PRESS
New York / Ramsey

Unless otherwise acknowledged, all Bible passages are translated from the German as freely quoted or paraphrased by Eberhard Arnold. The Bible references are added by the editors.

Library of Congress Catalog Card Number: 83-62952

ISBN: 0-8091-2609-5

Published by Paulist Press
545 Island Road, Ramsey, N.J. 07446

Printed and bound in the
United States of America

Contents

PEACE AND THE RULE OF GOD

In memory of our beloved brother and sister
Heini and Annemarie Arnold

Acknowledgments

Two things sparked this publication. One was the wish of Eberhard Arnold's son Heini, our late Elder, to commemorate the hundredth anniversary of his father's birth. The other was the long-standing request of John Farina, associate editor of Paulist Press, to publish a book about the Bruderhof. His constant encouragement and reassurance deserve special thanks.

After the first selection of material had been made, John Howard Yoder, professor at the University of Notre Dame and the Associated Mennonite Biblical Seminaries of Elkhardt, Indiana, joined the editing team with his invaluable services as consultant. Our warm thanks go to him for writing the Introduction and for reviewing the selection process and the outline.

Our appreciations go to our neighbor in England, the well-known author and TV commentator Malcolm Muggeridge, who wrote the Preface in spite of his very busy schedule and advanced age; and to our friend Vincent Harding for his help and advice.

Our gratitude goes to two early members of the Bruderhof: Else von Hollander and Günther Homann, who with others faithfully preserved and catalogued the articles and the lecture and meeting transcripts from which this book was extracted. It is a small miracle that, after years of persecution, flight, and pioneering in the subtropics, we still have this material in our archives.

Preface

One of the very pleasant happenings in Robertsbridge since my wife Kitty and I came to live there some twenty-five years ago has been the arrival in the village of the Society of Brothers. They took over what had been a tuberculosis sanatorium, Darvell Hall, no longer needed for lack of patients, and soon got it into shape to accommodate their community. There was to begin with a good deal of speculation about them among the villagers, and some standoffishness because they were strangers, quite a number of whom spoke with a strong American accent. Their good nature, their readiness to help in any way, their smiles and friendliness, soon overcame this, and they became, not just tolerated, but affectionately regarded.

The Brothers, as we learned, along with their wives and children, came originally from Germany, where they belonged to a Christian movement under the auspices of Eberhard and Emmy Arnold, whose aim was to make possible living in community like the early Christians, self-supporting, holding their goods in common, each family having its own quarters wherein to bring up their children, but all worshiping and praying together. Eberhard's writings very simply and beautifully describe this way of life, as it were, little oases of peace and love in a turbulent world.

Curiously enough, as a child I was confronted with a

somewhat similar experiment in communal living. This was the Whiteway Colony, in the Cotswolds near Stroud, where some early Socialists, among them friends of my father, had banded together, bought some acres of land to cultivate, and set themselves to live together in a community in which money, marriage, and private property had been abolished. The adventure began with ceremonially burning the title deeds of their land and ended with establishing squatters' rights to it. As for abolishing marriage—alas, they had not also abolished adultery, and much confusion and bitterness ensued. Money likewise, though abolished, kept turning up and making mischief. The original inspiration of the colonists came from Tolstoy's writings, which, with all their splendor, lacked the power of the Gospels to hold the enterprise together.

Again, when I was a newspaper correspondent in Washington, D.C., I came across the Mennonites, whom I greatly admired for their detachment from the standard American way of life and who had given the Brothers a helping hand when the exigencies of the 1939–1945 war made it necessary for them to cross the Atlantic. John Wesley noted down in his diary that when he converted someone, he became industrious, abstemious, and honest, and so was liable to become rich, whereupon all the work was to do again. The Mennonites, and also the Brothers, might well fit into this scenario, and so should watch out.

In the story of Christendom, the monastic orders have functioned as a sort of lightning conductor, preventing Christ's Kingdom of love from being destroyed in the storms and earthquakes to which the kingdoms of the world are subject in their pursuit of power, in their adoration of Vanity Fair and acceptance of Nietzsche's pronouncement just before he finally went mad: "God is dead; long live superman!"

What St. Francis was to the Franciscans and St. Benedict to the Benedictines, Eberhard Arnold is to the Brothers, showing them how they may live together, work together, marry and bring up their families together, thereby not separating themselves as drastically as the traditional monks and nuns did and do, but still living with and in Christ, still faithfully walking with God, rather than being caught up in the Gadarene rush in which the so-called free world seems to be bent. Their worst hazard, as it seems to me, is not that they might be lured away from their community, but that they might fall for the illusion that peace movements promote peace, or that some earthly fantasy like Socialism can enable us to live happily ever after; forgetful that our Lord rejected the Devil's offer of the kingdoms of the world and chose rather to die on His Cross.

The children of the Brothers give special delight; their eyes express the wonder of life rather than the fantasies of a TV screen, and their voices, when they sing, harmonize with the birds. In our village we rejoice that they should be with us.

Robertsbridge, East Sussex   *Malcolm Muggeridge*
July 1983

Introduction

Emmy Arnold stood outside her husband Eberhard's study, ready to face the Gestapo. Eberhard lay on the couch, his broken leg in a cast, watching his sister-in-law burn potentially incriminating papers in the stove. Meanwhile, 140 Nazi storm troopers and secret police were searching the little community in the Rhön hills for non-existent arms and anti-Nazi literature. It was eight o'clock in the morning of November 16, 1933, in Hitler's Germany. Late that evening one of the Gestapo's big cars drove off full of books and papers.

We commemorate in 1983 the hundredth birthday of a man whose work seemed smashed at fifty. Eberhard Arnold was crippled by a leg injury from which he never was to recover (his death came two years later from the complications of attempted corrective surgery). His ambitious publishing program was ended in midstream by the seizure of his office and the tightening coils of Nazi censorship. His energies in those last two years were to be drained by shepherding his refugee household into Switzerland, Liechtenstein, England . . .

But that was not the end. The Bruderhof movement, though decapitated, cut down, and scattered, did not wither away but grew up again, and again, in England, in Paraguay, in the United States . . .

That 1933 was not the end, but only the middle of a story,

we owe not to the man but to his living witness. It is that witness which this book documents, by gathering and ordering fragments, mostly previously unpublished, from his writing and teaching.

An introduction could seek to summarize what follows in the book. I shall not do that. An introduction could seek to explain why what follows is important, or why it is true. That I shall not do either. I shall attempt rather to locate Arnold, to put him on the map, to make understandable to American readers in the 1980's what the causes and the cultural currents were which, in 1899 or 1907, in 1919 or 1932, fed into the new global vision which the following texts in this book exposit. Other narratives of the life of Eberhard Arnold himself and that of the Bruderhof are already available. We seek here only to recount enough so that the reader unfamiliar with their story can understand the world from which and into which Arnold came, and identify the issues to which these texts originally spoke.

Eberhard Arnold saw himself as servant of a vision which he did not invent, herald of a cause incommensurably greater than his service to it. That vision had come together from many sources, borne toward him by many people and movements. The reader who is less interested in backgrounds and origins may prefer to read Arnold directly, as he himself seeks to read the Gospel with unvarnished immediacy.

From before the First World War into the late 1920's, Arnold was a popular figure on the lecture circuit in Germany, serving universities, the youth movement world, and the student Christian world. Notes or outlines of many of these talks have been preserved in rough form. From early 1920 until his death in 1935 Arnold was regularly presenting teaching sessions for the members and the guests of his community. From many of these talks as well, rough notes have been retained. It is from these sources that most of the following materials have been drawn. The talks have been reconstituted and translated by the labors of the archive workers at Woodcrest, selected (with the advice of many others in the community) with a view to their not overlapping with the already available writings of Arnold and yet presenting an independently coherent picture of his teachings. In this process I have aided as "editor" only in an a posteriori and honorific sense, reviewing with the Woodcrest staff their decisions as to which fragments to retain and as to what explanation is needed.

The texts we have before us are not the preferred point of entrance to the devotional or spiritual guidance of Arnold. That would be his *Inner Land*, written in the face of the spiritual crisis which Germany faced in World War I, and expanded since then in several editions until his death. Nor are the following texts all the heart of his message. That, Arnold himself would probably have said, was his *Salt and Light*, his interpretation of the Sermon on the Mount, not because of any great originality but because of its simplicity and because he was convinced that his movement had its heart not in himself but in the person and teaching of Jesus. Nor can it be a survey of the breadth of things he taught and wrote about, which extended from secular philosophy, ancient and modern, into political economy and the arts.

What we have here is rather a selection of those dominant strands of Arnold's instruction which will most faithfully and adequately portray to the reader the source and rationale of the life of the community which has survived him for half a century by listening attentively to his both simple and prophetic pastoral instruction. That the selection is fitting for that purpose is guaranteed by the means used to prepare it. The initial choice of passages to reproduce was done by a wide consultation involving most of the senior members of the Woodcrest community. At least a half-dozen community members shared in the task of translating into English those fragments which had not already appeared in English. At least fifteen couples contributed to the process of choosing which texts they thought most distinctive and representative. The passages chosen were then honed and ordered by the team of several workers who devote part of their time to the community archives. The resulting collections have also been reread in plenary assemblies. Thus while every word is from Eberhard's teaching or writing and over a half-century old, the text is also the living witness of the Society of Brothers.

The topic choices and the judgments as to how much of which texts belonged in which place were made in that internal discipline of the community's own memory bank. An outsider might have selected other fragments as more original, or less familiar, or farther from the awareness of the reader. That selection would not have spoken in the same way of the living memory which is sustained by and which sustains the witness of the Society of Brothers as organism.

My responsibility as editorial consultant has not included reaching back into the original texts, nor finding other texts in the untranslated sources which might be more interesting. I have merely reviewed some of the final stages of selection and translation in order to help the original thrust of a text come through as adequately as possible. We have sought to have the voice be that of Arnold himself and not of his disciples a half-century later, yet we recognize that distinction to be intrinsically impossible. It is the people still living in the life which he founded who are most able to be custodians of his memory, even if the guardianship itself may unavoidably and usually unconsciously soften the differences beween founder and followers. Such a telescoping of a man into his memory, as sustained by his followers' followers, happened to Jesus and St. Francis. My concern as editorial observer has not been to keep it from happening to Arnold.

A bibliography is provided for the reader who might be interested to pursue the history of one or another of these earlier traditions and movements from which Arnold drew and the history and witness of the Bruderhof movement itself. Detailed source identification for the Arnold texts (mostly previously unpublished) is held to a minimum, with only as much annotation amidst the materials as is needed to make them understandable.

Teenage Convert: 1899

Our picture of the religious heritage of most of Germany for centuries was of unrelieved established Lutheran orthodoxy, allying university, pulpit, government, and bourgeoisie in unchanging and uninteresting fidelity. That was all there, but it was not all there was. There was the heritage of the frontier American revival movement of Charles G. Finney, under whose impact Eberhard's great-grandfather John Arnold had come, resulting in Eberhard's grandparents, Franklin Luther and Maria Arnold, née Ramsauer, being sent from America to Africa as missionaries. For the sake of education Eberhard's father Carl Franklin was taken as a boy into an upper class home in Bremen, where the devotional heritage of pietist pastors Collenbusch and Menken was honored. In young Eberhard's world in Breslau, the city to whose university his father was called as professor of Church history, there was the Salvation Army, whose workers' involvement with the poor struck him as more morally authentic than his family's social life. There was his "uncle" (husband of his mother's cousin) Ernst Ferdinand Klein, who as Lutheran pastor in a working-class community had sided with the workers of the weaving industry, in such a way that his critics had prevailed upon the church administration to transfer him to a small town in the outskirts of Berlin. There were members of the Moravian pietist tradition and of the new "fellowship movement" putting their fingers on the need for personal conversion.

From the outset, spiritual authenticity was linked in Eberhard's mind with awareness of economic injustice. His earliest memory of this linkage was his discomfort at the occasion of his own confirmation ceremony; it struck him that he and the other youths of his class had beautiful new clothing for the occasion, while others had to wear their weekday best.

The seeds for a desperate struggle to find the living Christ were laid during a summer vacation at Uncle Ernst's home. It was here that Eberhard began reading the Gospels with the same excitement and fascination that had formerly been provided by Karl May's adventure novels. He needed to know who this Jesus really was. Back home in Breslau, he sought out a young pastor for guidance and was given the advice not to rest until he had found the answer.

Eberhard knew that there were areas in his life that were not Christ-like. It was a struggle for him to recognize Christ as Lord of everything: his superficial relationships with fellow-students, among whom he had played a somewhat prominent role; his disrespect for teachers; and not least the newly aroused physical passions that assaulted him.

It was October 1899 when the sixteen-year-old, praying alone in the comfortable family parlor, reached both the inner assurance of God's forgiving grace toward him and the resolve outwardly to confess his new faith and joy. Both the overtness of his piety and the bluntness of his social concern caused tension even within his own family. Most memorable was his daring to reprimand his parents for the partying which belonged to the duties of their class:

Father, I hear that the food and drink for this party costs more than two hundred marks. Those invited are almost all richer than we are. They all have enough to eat at home. They will invite you again and will offer you wine, roast meat, and ices, which are just as costly. I know of poor innocent families in the east end of the city, who have not enough money to provide their little children with sufficient milk. You know what Jesus said, "When you give a feast, do not invite your acquaintances and friends, who in turn can invite you; but rather go out on the streets and invite the poorest people who cannot invite you." You go to Church and hold morning prayers; but is this unjust life from God or from the Devil? (*Seeking for the Kingdom,* p. 27).

Decisive Commitments: 1907

Since the 1520's the agenda of spiritual renewal in Protestantism had seldom avoided surfacing the issue of baptism upon confession of faith. In the sixteenth century, the people who renewed the practice of linking baptism with the conversion or adult personal faith of the candidate were called "Anabaptists." Usually such action meant the creation of new Church bodies, as had been the case for the "Anabaptists" of the continental sixteenth century or the "Baptists" of the British seventeenth century. It however happened more recently in the context of pietistic revival preaching and pastoring that persons of solidly religious background and upbringing came to the conviction that they needed, as adults, to express the wholeness and joy of their newfound faith by requesting baptism, without creating a new Church body. They felt that the faith they had now come to know was of an utterly new quality contrasted to the way in which their "Christening" as products of established Christianity had made them participants in a culture but not in a faith. Eberhard was prepared along both of these lines to face the issue of baptism as a young adult. His father had already spoken to him of the sixteenth-century Anabaptist movement, whose nearly buried traces in Protestant history were just beginning to be rediscovered by historians. Eberhard met as well the representatives of the other strand: the lawyer-evangelist Ludwig von Gerdtell (1872–1954, founder of the European Evangelistic Society), arguing that it is proper to express one's adult Christian commitment in the act of baptism upon confession of faith without intending that act to mean sectarian separation. Middle class circles in the city of Halle, where Eberhard had studied theology, were being shaken by von Gerdtell's lectures and stirred by Bible study meetings held in homes. There Eberhard met the sisters Else and Emmy von Hollander, daughters of a professor of law who had moved to Halle from Riga to escape the Russification of the Baltic nations. Within a month Emmy and Eberhard were engaged to marry.

Eberhard was a frequent speaker in those Bible study circles. To the step of baptism upon confession of faith first Else and then Eberhard and Emmy were led in 1908. That did not make them Baptists; even less did it make them Mennonites or Hutterites. It did not make them members of any local church. It simply committed them to a life of discipleship whose meaning in detail they would have been the first to say they were in no position to predict. Three quarters of a century later, with the perspective of Eberhard's further estrangement from established Protestantism and rapprochement to the heirs of the Anabaptist movement, we can speak in one way of these baptisms in 1908 as the first step on that path. Yet if the three young friends had been told that it was that, would they have taken it?

Eberhard was told formally, before his baptism, that it would disqualify him for the theological degree and pastoral office toward which he had been studying. He studied instead for a philosophical doctorate. His dissertation on the thought of Friedrich Nietzsche was accepted in November 1909, and in December he and Emmy were married. He worked as freelance lecturer for the Fellowship Movement.

The Student Christian Movement

The Anglo-Saxon revival movement of which the American Dwight L. Moody was a major spokesman soon found a new form of organization befitting its social level and its world mission. Taking off from the similar "non-church" foundation laid by the Young Men's Christian Association (German CVJM organized on a national level in 1883), the Student Christian Movement was able, thanks to its special social location, to avoid both antagonizing the established churches and being roped in by them. John R. Mott (1865-1955), the worldwide ambassador of the Moody revival, which had broken into the student world at Northfield (Massachusetts) in 1886, had visited Germany's university cities in 1898. Its stated goals of "deepening Christian life through common prayer and Bible study as well as the fostering of Christian work among its members and other students" were pursued without direct attention to Church structures.

The SCM was the context of young Dr. Arnold's first public notoriety. As freelance lecturer he spoke at campuses on such themes as "Early Christianity in the Present" and "Jesus As He Really Was"—presaging his lifelong focus upon the Gospels and the earliest Christians. In 1915 he became editor of *The Furrow,* the periodical (soon a publishing house) of the SCM. World War I called the SCM into relief services and special publications in the interest of soldiers. Called to military service but discharged for health reasons after a few weeks' service as a quartermaster corps wagon driver, Arnold had seen enough of war to begin moving toward what soon became a convinced Christian pacifism. It was his pastoral talks with soldiers in the hospital that convinced him that war could not be right.

The SCM provided the constituency, the mix of spiritual simplicity and intellectual seriousness, the meld of flexibility and organizational sobriety, which were to launch Arnold into the 1920's.

The "Religious-Social Movement"

It is not clear when Arnold came in touch with this most important stream of renewal concern within German Protestantism. At least by the end of the First World War he had become fully acquainted with its contribution. It had represented in the last quarter of the nineteenth century a set of dramatic new beginnings, some of which fed into the revitalization of the mainline churches, but several of which were not satisfied with that objective.

The movement represents a most unique synthesis of components which in the Anglo-Saxon experience are often not held together: pietism and social concern. By "pietism" here is meant minimally the readiness to use that term as a self-designation, or to accept it from others. This located the people I shall be describing within a two-centuries-old stream of minority renewal concern. More substantially, the term identifies the conviction that there is a dimension of reality in the encounter with the living God in prayer, guidance, and miracle, which can and must be affirmed rather than outgrown as we build community.

The ministry of Johann Christoph Blumhardt (1805–1880) had begun when as a young pastor he was participant, to his own surprise, in an event of exorcism which freed a young woman from a depressive possession. Under the motto "Jesus is victor" Blumhardt developed over the next half century a ministry of pastoral care to individuals coming from all over the country, in which he was succeeded by his son, Christoph Friedrich. Yet (in a way quite distinct from the individualistic or internalistic turn which such deliverance ministries can take) the proclamation of Christ's lordship meant for the Blumhardts a claim laid upon all of life including the social and political. Christoph in fact became a member of the social democratic party and for one term a member of Württemberg's parliament.

The spiritual and intellectual successors of the Blumhardts arose not in Germany but in Switzerland, in a small circle of theologians calling themselves "social-religious": Leonhard Ragaz (1868–1945), Hermann Kutter (1863–1931), and Karl Barth (1886–1968). These men differed among themselves—later they differed bitterly—about just how to connect Gospel faith and Christian social commitment; but for all three the link was essential, a matter of the Kingdom of God and not merely of debatable social analysis. Kutter was the first of the three to become known, with books like his *Justice: An Old Word to Modern Christendom* (of 1905). Arnold later said that the first half of his spiritual pilgrimage had led him "from Luther to Kutter."

The Youth Movement

The collapse of a culture's hallowed values is for no one more upsetting than for youth. What lost the war for Germany in 1918 was not just an imperial dynasty and a military command structure; it was a civilization, the proud self-confidence of middle-class urbanity. Their elders, though defeated and demoralized, went on living; but what should youth be looking

forward to? Some turned to nihilism, some to political radical-
ity of left or right, but a broad current of German youth took
another path; they went walking. The movement was not a
new invention; it had begun at the turn of the century under
such names as "Birds of Passage" (*Wandervögel*) and "Free
Youth"; they had taken on causes from anti-alcoholism to
school reform. Thus by 1918 there was a backlog of "adults"
waiting from the pre-war movement and a new pool of thousands looking for new answers. What arose with a surge of new
energy in the immediate post-war period, coming to be called
simply "the youth movement," was a new joy in nature, folk
singing and dancing, walking and camping, non-politicized
and non-eroticized friendships, and clean fun, overcoming
class disparities through simplicity linked with disrespect for
materialism and social stuffiness. Half a century later, American youth were to call something like this "the spirit of Wood-
stock," but there was in the German movement no
generational anger, and no drugs. A decade later the movement was vulnerable to co-option in the Nazi "national renewal," but there was none of that racist nationalism in the
beginnings. Within the youth movement the specifically Christian witness of the fellowship movements found an open audi-
ence, whereas established parish religion (what Arnold was
now calling the "world church") had lost their respect.

Synthesis

What happened in 1919–1921 was the flowing together of
"all the above" in a powerful new mixture, with Eberhard Arnold in the middle of it all. The first post-war Pentecost re-
gional conference of the SCM was held at Marburg, June
13–15, 1919, dominated by Arnold's charismatically clear and
urgent expositions of the Sermon on the Mount and by his

"Communism: Summons to Christianity." A participant at the Marburg conference reported:

> The focus of all that was said and thought was Jesus' Sermon on the Mount. Eberhard Arnold burned it into our hearts with a passionate spirituality, hammered it into our wills with prophetic power and the tremendous mobile force of his whole personality. This was the Sermon on the Mount in the full force of its impact, in its absolute and undiminished relevance, its unconditional absoluteness (Erwin Wissman, quoted in *Salt and Light,* p. x).

That fall (September 22–25) saw at Tambach in Thuringia an encounter with the leadership of the Swiss "religious social" movement. Karl Barth was the most prominent of the Swiss speakers. Arnold became editor of the movement's journal *Das neue Werk* whose subtitle, "The Christian in the People's State," expressed the vision that not only piety but also society would be swept into the Kingdom movement. The next Pentecost conference (May 21, 1920 at Schlüchtern, northeast of Frankfurt) multiplied the momentum, and by the following fall it was reported that "Schlüchtern fellowships" were forming in the major cities and universities.

In addition to his traveling ministry of public speeches and his editing of movement periodicals, Arnold initiated an ambitious project of the republication of Christian sources, representing the vision of renewal over the centuries. Volumes were published from the writings of Tertullian, Augustine, Francis of Assisi, Jacob Böhme, Zinzendorf, Sören Kierkegaard, and Dostoevsky, among others. Additional projects that included Bernard of Clairvaux, the early Anabaptists, Martin Luther, George Fox, John Bunyan, Fénelon, William and Catherine Booth, and Pascal could not be completed. Arnold's own collection of testimonies from "the early Christians after the death of the apostles" (published 1926) was one of his major projects.

As is natural in such times of fermentation, institutional changes were rapid. Publications were initiated, renamed, divided. The leadership of the Student Christian Movement and its publication arm, "The Furrow," divided. Old friendships were strained and new alliances sealed, some to break again.

Antithesis

Before there was time to be comfortable amidst this new power and popularity, Arnold was led to his next step, the creation of economic and residential community. The first nucleus began moving to Sannerz, near Schlüchtern, late in 1920. By mid-1922, when it faced its first internal crisis, the commune had grown to forty members, not all of whom were as convinced as Arnold of the possibility of complete community. Not all were ready with him to see "faith" as meaning not only current sharing but trusting that God would provide for all future needs. Again the publishing work was split up; again old friendships were strained. From that crisis came the *Bruderhof* life form which has since undergone no substantial change. Arnold had begun his second major shift, which he categorized as "from Kutter to Hutter."

Continuity

Already when Arnold was young his father had spoken to him about the radical Protestants of earlier European history who on the one hand, the father thought, were the only true Christians, and yet had been discredited by the fact that God had not blessed them with prosperity but had permitted their cause almost to die out. That had been Eberhard's introduction to the fact that there had been within Protestant history an undercurrent of more committed Protestantism than the one dominating Germany. In the Hutterian communities of the American prairie states and provinces Arnold found the descendants of those ancient movements.

The so-called "Anabaptist" movement of the sixteenth century had radicalized the biblical renewal vision of Luther and Zwingli to the point of rejecting religious establishment, warfare, and infant baptism. This movement had survived through the sixteenth century, especially in the upper Rhine basin (there are Mennonites in Switzerland, Alsace, and Württemberg to this day) and in the Netherlands. From there, their descendants had migrated in the eighteenth century to America and to Russia. A third center survived even more effectively in Moravia, where the so-called Hutterian brethren created the commune pattern called Bruderhof. It was the heirs of this third group, all of whom emigrated from imperial Russia in the 1870's, that Arnold sought out in western Canada in 1930, in order to ally his new beginnings with the heirs of the oldest beginnings.

Other radical Reformation phenomena also were known to Arnold. He in fact published new editions of the writings of some of them, and planned to publish more. But the Czech Brethren of the fifteenth century had been wiped out in the seventeenth. The heirs of the Waldensians from the twelfth century had made their peace with Calvinism in 1534. It was therefore with the Hutterian movement that it seemed most fitting for the alliance of old and new disciples to be concluded.

Arnold spent a year in 1930–31 establishing that connection, visiting all Bruderhof colonies existing at that time in the United States and Canada. In December 1930 the congregation at Macleod, Alberta welcomed him into their membership and commissioned him as their missionary to Europe.

The commonality between the old and the new Bruderhof went beyond the basic Anabaptist convictions of believers' baptism and non-resistance, and beyond the communal economic pattern of the Bruderhof. The Hutterian Brethren of the sixteenth century had been pioneers in the creation of elementary schools for all children; likewise Arnold's movement had since the beginnings at Sannerz taken advantage of the facilities offered by communal residence to operate an alternative school, not only for their own offspring but also for needy children to whom the Bruderhof provided foster care, and for others whose parents preferred such a familial and religiously oriented schooling. The Bruderhof regularly counted on members with qualification for teaching. Numerous of Arnold's writings (represented only minimally in this collection) were devoted to the values of familially based holistic education. They help refute the notion, current in some sociological circles, that Anabaptism is not concerned for culture.

Although Arnold was correct in seeing that the link established with the older Hutterite movement represented a kind of spiritual validation for his new beginning, and a chance for his community to receive both correction and moral support, it would have been wrong if he had thought, as some observers think he might have thought, that this connection, which in the 1930's only existed in his person, would provide for the European communities a decision-making structure, an identity and spiritual leadership to meet all future questions. In Arnold's absence, leadership styles in the communities were to change more than once in the next half century in ways that need not be narrated when our concern is to understand Arnold himself. The mutual affirmation between the new European communities and the Hutterites was little more than symbolic as the core group migrated to England and then to Paraguay. After the first colonies were founded in the United States, the amount of interchange decreased rather than increasing. In

1955 the relationship was suspended, and then was restored on a new basis in 1974.

Transition

The story begins to end where our account began. There was no chance that Nazism could tolerate the Bruderhof. After the Gestapo break-in of November 16, 1933, steps were taken to remove all children to Switzerland, so that when a new Nazi schoolteacher arrived in January 1934 there were no Bruderhof children for him to teach. Arnold contacted Mennonites in the Netherlands and Friends in England; some English members joined the Bruderhof, and the groundwork was laid for an English colony to be formed in 1936. But Arnold's shepherd-teacher ministry was ending. The near-daily devotional Bible studies and the discussions, from the records of which many of the fragments in this collection come, were coming to an end, as his wide-ranging popular lecturing had a decade before. The foundation had been laid.

From His Time to Ours

We cannot see, in 1983, how this world can go on. There is growing conflict between the hungry South and the wasteful North. There is the snowballing nuclear threat between the superpowers (crossing just this fall another threshold of de-stabilizing technological "progress"). Within each culture tensions between generations, sexes, ethnic groups are exacerbated. Again loud voices advocate desperate measures which are not solutions: violent insurrection, waging a nuclear war, self-sufficient "survival," suicide.

Then we remember how it was the collapse of national cultural self-confidence which freed German youth in 1919–21 to be seized in an unprecedented way by the power of

Jesus' Kingdom message. We remember how it was the collapse of democracy and the rise of Hitler which set in bold relief *how* different and how powerful is the *corporate* quality of spiritual resistance. We remember that it was in the desperation of the late first century that the Apostle John was given visions of how God's saving purposes for the world are not thwarted but enhanced by that setting. Thus our discerning more frankly the wounds and the wars of our world of the 1980's, which Arnold could not foresee, may once again set in relief the pertinence and the promised power of the Kingdom way, the course already set for us, which the following texts so simply and so authentically interpret.

Vancouver   *John Howard Yoder*
July 26, 1983

THIS CRUMBLING WORLD AND GOD'S COMING ORDER

Eberhard and Emmy Arnold, Whitsun, 1921

On the Edge of Catastrophe

We seem, to our horror, to be standing on the brink of a catastrophic judgment. It is so close that it can be averted only through God's direct intervention.

Worship meeting, Rhön Bruderhof, Sept. 2, 1935

The human race has made stupendous technological progress, conquering time and space by means of automobiles and airplanes; but how many thousands of people are being killed by these very same means! There are amazing achievements in the big cities, yet most urban families die out in the third or fourth generation.

The most sinister powers of our civilization are the three mighty organizations—the State, the military, and the capitalist structure. These three organizations represent the highest achievement of the earth spirit. The tremendous edifice built up by a fallen creation is incredible. But it will end in death. How mighty is this power, how unquestioned its apparent worth!

Meeting with guests, Alm Bruderhof, Sept. 16, 1934

The dark reality of today—humankind destroying and ruining itself in reiterated madness—must be opposed by a much greater reality: the light of tomorrow. In this light humankind is called to something that is the opposite of betrayal and deception, of murder and hate, of death and destruction. (1 Thess. 5:4–5)

But we will not find the assurance that the dawn is coming until we have grasped night's darkness, its impenetrable blackness and bottomless suffering.

Public lecture, Berlin, Apr. 7, 1919

The rule of evil affects all human beings. In our day it has reached massive proportions. We come across it in every form of government, in every Church, in every gathering no matter how pious, in all political parties and labor unions, even in family life and in our Brotherhood. It has a demonic power that shows up in every one of these structures, however different they may be on the surface. They are pervaded by the inclination to obstinate self-determination, the tendency to present what is one's own as the only thing that counts—one's own person, one's own nation, State, Church, sect, party, labor union, one's own family or community—or at least, one's own way of thinking.

"Die Revolution Gottes," Die Wegwarte, 1926

There has hardly ever been a time when it was as evident as it is today that God and His righteousness and love do not yet rule. We see it in our own lives and in current events. We see it in the fate of the hopeless, the millions upon millions of unemployed. We see it in the unjust distribution of goods though the earth offers unstintingly its fertility and all its potentials. There is urgent work that must be done to help humankind, but it is obstructed and destroyed by the injustice of the present world systems.

We are in the midst of a collapse of civilization. Civilization is nothing but humankind's orderly work in nature. And this work has turned into a disorder whose injustice cries out to heaven.

There are hundreds of signs that something is about to happen. Nothing in history takes place, however, unless it comes from God. So our plea to Him now is that He make history, His history, the history of His righteousness. And when God makes His history, we all have every reason to tremble. For as matters stand today, He can do nothing unless His wrath first sweeps over all the injustice and lovelessness, all the discord and brutality, that rule the world. His wrath will be the beginning of His history. First must come the day of judgment; then the day of joy, of love, grace, and justice can dawn.

But if we ask God to intervene, we must bare our own breasts before Him so that His lightning can strike us, for we are all guilty. There is no one who is not guilty of the wickedness in today's world.

Rhön Bruderhof, 1933

No one can deny that the revolutionary movements have aroused the human conscience, thus violently shaking humanity's soul. The conscience cannot find peace until its warning cry reaches into every person's life. The attack by socialism and communism on the status quo is a call to our consciences—those of us who consider ourselves Christians. This call warns us more strongly than any sermon that our task is to live in active protest against everything that opposes God in this world. So poorly have we Christians filled this role that the question must be asked: Are we Christians at all?

"Jesus und der Zukunftsstaat,"
unpublished article, 1919

Every awakening of humankind's collective conscience is of deep significance. There is such a thing as a world conscience, the conscience of humanity. It rises up against war and bloodshed, against mammonism and social injustice, against violence of any kind.

Public lecture, Berlin, Apr. 7, 1919

At this eleventh hour hearts must be made ready, through faith, to receive the powers of the future world, the Spirit of the upper Jerusalem. (Rev. 3:10–12)

The final Kingdom is near, and the whole world should be on the watch. But the world will not take heed unless the Church of Jesus Christ puts the unity and justice of this Kingdom into practice daily. Faith will bring about true unity among believers who are ready to live a life of unlimited, active love.

Alm Bruderhof leaflet, May 1934

He has called us, not so that we love our own lives, not even the lives of our fellow human beings. In other words, we are called to live, not for people, but for the honor of God and His Kingdom. We must not endeavor to raise ourselves to God's Kingdom by loving our life and taking good care of it. The way to the Kingdom leads through death, through very real death. It demands that our life be given up for the sake of God and His Kingdom. (Mark 8:35)

If we understand our time as it really is, we cannot fail to see how close that demand has come. We need not even go so far as to think of war, though it seems imminent. The political situation today requires that we be willing at any moment to lose our lives in serving the cause we have taken up. And woe to those who try again and again to keep their lives! (John 12:25)

Meeting with guests, Rhön Bruderhof, Sept. 13, 1935

Wake up, you who sleep, and arise; then Christ will reach you! (Rom. 13:11) The call is meant for anyone who has slipped back into the gloomy twilight of his own heart: "Wake up and arise from the dead!" Christ, the true Light, stands before you. (Eph. 5:14) He will strengthen you so that you may do powerful deeds, the deeds of love that are born solely of faith in Christ.

You are living in the end-time. "It is the last hour." (1 John 2:18) See to it that you lead a blameless life. That means you must look to the future and shape your life in accordance with God's future. Make use of the present moment, for the times are evil. The hour of extreme danger has come. People must wake up if they look for protection in the coming judgment. Therefore do not be foolish. Learn to understand the will of the Most High in our day. (Eph. 5:15–17) Be alert in these evil and dangerous times, lest in the hour of temptation you remain under the judgment. The foolish virgins became careless. You too will come to grief in the coming judgment unless you can borrow or are given oil for your lamps. (Matt. 25:1–13)

Rhön Bruderhof, July 26, 1931

The Kingdom Breaking In

If in all we do we have no other goal than this: that His Kingdom come, that His will be done on earth, then our prayer will be answered. (Matt. 6:33) God will prove greater than our hearts can grasp. Much more will happen than we dare put into words. His answer will surpass our boldest prayer. And so that we may be sure it is God who does it all, it will happen while we are yet praying or even before we have spoken our prayer. (Isa. 65:24) Anyone who knocks at God's door and seeks God alone will receive what he asks for before he knows it. (Matt. 7:7–11)

1929; English translation: Prayer Life, *pp. 24–25*

Let us ask God to send forth His Spirit with renewed authority. New thoughts must break forth from the depths of God's heart that go far, far beyond our own human thoughts and weak notions. Let us pray for God's mighty deeds, deeds that are completely independent of us human beings. Our prayer is that His rulership really break in, that His love be revealed, that His Kingdom become visible, ready for the Holy Spirit and Christ to descend. To this we will give ourselves, even if it costs us our lives. We will pledge our lives that this may come about for the deliverance of all nations.

Worship meeting, Rhön Bruderhof, Sept. 1935

The miraculous powers of God, the reality of His Kingdom, will be revealed in your midst; for it is the Holy Spirit
who grips you and penetrates you and takes you into the
sphere of God's coming Kingdom. (Acts 2:17–21) The wind
that precedes the storm is part of it. The Holy Spirit belongs
to the day of judgment and redemption when the Kingdom
breaks in, even though He is the voice of God in the storm that
precedes God's rule. Every time this happens, confirming the
event we know as the founding of the apostolic Church in Jerusalem, it affects the entire world.

Worship meeting, Rhön Bruderhof, Sept. 2, 1935

We are a hundred and fifty people, young and old, and
each one has experienced a special leading. All these different
threads have led us to life in community, a goal common to us
all. It is in accord with God's future Kingdom. By this we
mean something that is earthly as well as heavenly. We believe
in life beyond, eternal life. But at the same time we believe in
life here on earth, the life that looks toward God's future, that
expects eternal powers to break in and conquer the earth for
God's coming Kingdom.

Because we hold that the Church of Christ is an embassy
of God's future reign, we believe that the communal Church
has to represent here and now the charter of the Kingdom to
come. We say, the Holy Spirit is a harbinger of God's future;
the Holy Spirit is the element of the great future. And that is
why the Church receives the Holy Spirit, not so as to figure
out a map or timetable of God's Kingdom to go by—far from
it—but so that its life may be guided by perfect love, in keeping with the Spirit.

Certainly this means that we are in a situation of crass opposition to the zeitgeist, the spirit of the age. We withstand
both the spirit of dictatorship and the liberal spirit that gives

free rein to evil and sin, that allows people's sensual nature to have its fling, so to speak. Both go in a wrong direction. So from every point of view we are untimely.

Meeting with guests, Alm Bruderhof, July 2, 1935

There will be no need for do's and don'ts, no need for tables of commandments or tablets of law. In this Kingdom everything will be regulated by inner rebirth and inward inspiration, under the rule of Christ's Spirit.

Worship meeting, Rhön Bruderhof, Sept. 2, 1935

Jesus challenged us to work while it is still day. (John 9:4) He compared His Kingdom to labor in a vineyard, the investment of entrusted money, the good use of every talent. If God's Kingdom is to transform this vale of tears into a place of joy, it has to be a realm of work. Work, and work alone, befits the destiny of the human spirit. By our nature as human beings we are called to a life of creativity. Healthy joy in life will be ours only through unclouded, loving fellowship in work.

"Jesus und der Zukunftsstaat,"
unpublished article, 1919

We have been given an important calling in the context of the tremendous struggle between two opposites. We are unworldly in that we deny recognition to mutual displacement and annihilation. Yet we are close to the world and to nature in that we acknowledge the constructive social force of mutual help and interdependence. And we do not exclude anybody. We believe that all human beings, whoever they may be, are drawn together by this deep-down sense of solidarity and mutual service. We believe that all, however deeply they may have sunk into darkness, do yet have a spark of light in the depths of their hearts. We believe that this spark of light in every person must in the end gather them all together in the ocean of light—fellowship with God.

Worship meeting, Alm Bruderhof, June 2, 1935

It is not uncommon to hear people say it is wrong to try to bring about prematurely any part of God's Kingdom. That is true. We human beings must not and cannot hasten into being what God will do. But by saying it is wrong to force anything, people tend all too often to cover up their lack of faith in the Holy Spirit. Men and women cannot precipitate God's Kingdom. But God can send a forerunner of his Kingdom: He sends the Holy Spirit, who is the essence of the future Kingdom, who speeds ahead to herald the coming reign.

Rhön Bruderhof, May 31, 1934

There have been many people on whose hearts the suffering of the world weighed heavily and who therefore knew that one day justice would have to come. But Jesus is the only one who, as well as implanting in us the longing for justice, gave us the Kingdom with its clarity and justice and showed us the way there.

Rhön Bruderhof, June 9, 1931

The State and the Church that supports it are, relatively speaking, the best things in the darkness. Until all this relative good is overthrown, God's Kingdom will not come.

The absolute good is the wedding feast of the Lamb and His Supper. (Rev. 19:7–9) We need not try to imagine what form it will take. We are not interested in exact descriptions or pictures. Our concern is for His joy and His unity to be made visible across the whole horizon. The entire earth shall be one Church of Christ, the whole earth will join in His wedding feast, and peace will reign in all the earth. Christ will be present everywhere. And to live in Church community means to be faithful in our expectation of that day and to work faithfully toward it. Every wedding, every wedding feast, shall be a symbol; every common mealtime shall be a sign of brotherhood.

Worship meeting, Alm Bruderhof, Aug. 19, 1934

Christ fulfills everything, for in Him everything is already fulfilled. Boundless joy is given to us when we turn away from the old life and find forgiveness for it, when we turn to a new life with courage to dare. That is the joy of the Gospel, the joy of the Holy Spirit, joy in the Lord, the joy that encompasses all of life because it springs from the eternal God. (Phil. 4:4) It is joy in the certainty that this same happiness belongs to all, that the future is the Lord's.

"Neues Leben," Das neue Werk, 1920/21

The coming down of God's Kingdom when Jesus gives this earth back to God on the day of the new creation will be something different. Our prayer shall call on God to bring this about. We cannot do it, not even with our faith. God alone can do it.

An awakening must come; but something still greater must come. Can you grasp this? Can you grasp it that something even greater than the early apostolic times must come, namely the Kingdom of God, which will change the whole world?

Worship meeting, Rhön Bruderhof, Feb. 25, 1935

Jesus in the Sermon on the Mount

We ought constantly to occupy our minds and hearts with the person of Jesus: who He is, what He said, how He lived, how He died, and what His resurrection means. We have to take in the full import of His words in the Sermon on the Mount (Matt. ch. 5–7) and in the parables, and we have to represent to all the world the same things He represented in His life.

Worship meeting, Rhön Bruderhof, Mar. 24, 1935

What the Kingdom of God means is made clear in the Sermon on the Mount, in the Lord's Prayer, and in the words, "Enter by the narrow gate!" This means, treat people as you wish them to treat you. This is generally overlooked. You will not be going the way of discipleship until you do for everybody all that you ask from God for yourself, that is, absolute social justice and the peaceable atmosphere of God's Kingdom. We are envoys of the coming Kingdom of God; we serve only one law, the law of His Spirit.

The Sermon on the Mount tells us what that means in practice. To anyone who is sincere about it, the way is plain. Of course, no one can go this way without grace. Jesus indicates this when He speaks of the tree and its vitality in connection with the Kingdom of God. He also speaks of the salt, meaning the entirely new nature bestowed on us in Christ and the Holy Spirit. Jesus says, "Unless your justice is better than that of the moralists and theologians, you cannot enter the Kingdom of God." And He also says, "Seek first the Kingdom of God and His justice."

To be submerged in the wind of the Holy Spirit—that is the new life. Its effect will encompass the whole world. We need to have faith that we live in a time of grace; for the tree is meant to spread over the whole earth. And all humankind gathers under this tree, in the shelter of this living tree.

It is not enough to recognize that Jesus is the friend of our hearts; we must prove our love. And Jesus tells us how to do this: "Those who love me will keep my word!" (John 14:15)

Meeting with guests, Rhön Bruderhof, Sept. 1935

To be ready for God's Kingdom does not mean to stop eating and drinking or to reject marriage; it means recognizing the signs of the times and living now as we shall live in the future Kingdom of God. But what will be the sign that God's Kingdom is about to come? We read the answer in Matthew 24:31 and Mark 13:27: "And He will send His messengers with a trumpet sounding afar, and they will gather together His elect from the four winds, from one end of heaven to the other." That is the sign of the second coming of Christ. The gathering together is the sign of Christ—"How much did I desire to gather you as a hen gathers her chickens under her wings." (Matt. 23:37)

Worship meeting, Alm Bruderhof, Aug. 19, 1934

Jesus says that your words must be your deeds, your faith for the future must be your present living. The salvation of Je-

sus Christ must be your life. In this way you will find the right
attitude to all people and all things. You will not judge, but
you will sense that people's lives are ruined by social injustice;
you will feel that all guilt represents humanity's moral decline.
So you will take care not to expose the holiest things to eyes
and ears that do not understand. You will try to see that others
have everything that you want for yourself. Do you need a
house or a bank account? Then make that possible for all.
Whatever you expect others to do for you, do the same for
them. Love your neighbor as yourself—that is truth and reality; it is the reality of Jesus. And right afterwards He tells us to
go in by the narrow gate, to go the narrow way. Beware of the
way of compromise, the way of the many, the broad way. Beware of false prophets. They speak of peace and work for
peace, but they are not free from the power of money, from
mammon, lying, and impurity. Anyone who is not completely
free of mammon should not speak of peace; otherwise he is a
false prophet. Mammon is the murderer from the beginning.
Whoever has not broken with mammon should not speak of
peace, since he is a participant in the unceasing war that destroys the dispossessed by the power of wealth and its posses-
sors.

Jesus concludes with the challenge: It is no use to hear
these words unless you also do them. The finest peace palace
will collapse unless it fully represents the will of Jesus. The
call of Jesus goes to the core, to the very heart: Leave everything and go my way. "Sell all that you have and give to the
poor. Go with me!" (Matt. 19:21; Luke 5:27)

Meeting with guests, Alm Bruderhof, Aug. 17, 1934

Our experience of personal salvation has to go hand in
hand with our expectation for the whole world. Otherwise we
are not completely at one with God. And this will not happen

until we are at one in the interests that the all-powerful, caring God has. Then we are truly at one.

Who are the blessed? They are those who stand before God as beggars begging for His Spirit; who have become beggars in the material as well as the spiritual. They are those who are beggarly poor in goods and in grace. Only the beggarly poor know that to hunger and thirst means to agonize in this desire. Yet these are the truly blessed, who are plagued by this hunger and thirst for righteousness, who bear deep pain, who suffer the ultimate need, as Jesus suffered the ultimate need. Just as He suffered with the world's deepest suffering and in the bitterest God-forsakenness, only those are the blessed who suffer to the verge of death, for the world and its need. They have pure, clear, radiant hearts, they are concentrated on God's cause with completely undivided hearts, they are at one with God's heart and live from their hearts just as God lives from His heart. So they are the ones who bring peace in the midst of an unpeaceful and corrupted world.

Worship meeting, Rhön Bruderhof, Feb. 25, 1935

The New Testament says that faith does not depend on signs and wonders. Jesus says they should be kept secret. People too easily cling to miracles. So Jesus warns us not to speak of them or display them, because He wants us to find a faith that does not depend on miracles. (Luke 8:56)

Meeting with guests, Sept. 1935

Nowhere among the early Christians do we find the cold light of intellectual understanding that constantly analyzes and differentiates. Instead, there was the Spirit that burned within their hearts and made their souls alive. (Col. 2:8–10)

Bible study session, 1919

The crucial question is this: Do you believe in Christ? Do you love Christ?

It is no good to lament about our sins. What matters most is to believe in Christ and to love Christ. When we see the whole unhappy world going to pieces, when we realize how crazy it must sound to talk about faith and humanity and about being humane, then there can be no doubt: Christ alone remains the true Man, He who called Himself the Son of Man, the Child of Man.

There is nothing else for me to hold on to for my life or death, nothing else to believe in for my neighbors, for those who are close to my heart, nothing else to trust in for our Bruderhof, nothing else to hold on to for a world going to pieces. I have to confess: I have absolutely nothing but Christ alone! (Phil. 3:8)

Members' meeting, Rhön Bruderhof, Oct. 31, 1935

The Kingdom of God

The Kingdom of God—what do these words mean? A kingdom or realm is a political system; it is the orderly structure of a people in the work they do and their public relationships. It is a national community held together by justice and solidarity. This is the kind of realm the prophet Isaiah had in mind when he foretold the Kingdom of God. (Isa. 9:6–7) Such a realm exists only where people are living in a lasting, binding order of justice in all relationships, a new order given to our human condition.

What is unique about the way Jesus has shown us is that no one but God is in authority, no one else has the right to say anything. So it is quite right to speak of God's kingly rule. God alone has the rulership. He alone is King. That is the Kingdom of God.

We know, of course, that this Kingdom has not yet come on this earth. Not only God has great power; the mighty national governments have great power; lying and impurity have great power. Forces that are entirely opposed to God assert themselves. The Kingdom of God is not yet realized in our day. If it were, nothing else would count.

For God's Kingdom to come, the personal intervention of God through Jesus Christ is needed through the renewal of the world, the rebirth of the planet Earth. The Apostle Peter says that fire will melt the earth, and then the earth will be made completely new. (2 Pet. 3:12–13) And John the Evangelist says that in the new realm of God's kingship the earth will be so completely transformed that the sun is no longer needed, for there will be nothing but light. (Rev. 21:23)

Rhön Bruderhof, July 1, 1934

I believe that a radiation really went out from Jesus, that people accepted it with real thankfulness for their personal salvation and healing; but then they were satisfied. Their longing cooled off, and they were happy to be on the way to salvation, whereas that was actually only the start. Jesus says we must be born again in order to be included in the Kingdom of God, and He shows what the Kingdom of God means.

Here is where the interest dies down. People seek constant confirmation of such grace as they have already received. Instead they should say, "This personal experience is given to me to help me find clarity about the complete Christ and God's Kingdom, a clarity that will make my life part of the life for His Kingdom."

If the Kingdom of God is in the present as well as in the future, believers must be able to live here and now in accord with God's future Kingdom. Then their lives will also be in keeping with the historical life of Jesus Christ. Jesus Christ is the same yesterday, today, and to all Eternity, and we must become one with His life and His future by living today in accord with God's Kingdom and with the way it will be manifest in the future.

Meeting with guests, Rhön Bruderhof, Sept. 1935

People who want to assign to the Kingdom of God a place outside the actual history of the whole human race—as if it

were being prepared in a few converts only—ought surely to
find a new and broader vision through the mighty language
God speaks in history today. The increasing gravity of the
times makes it imperative for all who believe in the truth to
search the Scriptures and find out what the conditions for
God's Kingdom are and what effects it will have. We need to
be steeped in the biblical truth about God's Kingdom, so that
we can watch for the signs of the times and be found faithful
when He comes. (Matt. 16:3)

Der Hilfsbote, July 1915

God's economy, His plan for the Kingdom of God, must
be given well-defined practical expression in the household of
the Church. (Eph. 1:10; 3:9–11) Then even the blindest will
have to realize that here is a place where they can find something of the love and joy that God's Kingdom will bring to all
humankind at the end of time.

To those who ask us whether this is the only way people
can choose in order to bring down the Kingdom of God, we
say that it is not a way we choose. It is a way that comes down
to us from God. His economy, the plan He has for the human
race, is the highest and the only possible way. We human beings have no way that leads to the Kingdom of righteousness.
Unless God gives Himself to us, there is no way for us to go.

God comes down to us in His Church, created through
the outpouring of the Holy Spirit. The Church, the virgin
bride, who is our mother, comes to us, and all of life is transformed, including the economic structure. (Acts 2:1–4;
4:32–37)

Members's meeting, Rhön Bruderhof, July 3, 1933
(Cf. "Household Plan of God," in
Index of The Early Christians)

God's Kingdom is visible wherever Jesus is. That is why the First Letter of John begins with this testimony: What we have seen and heard, what we have touched with our hands, we proclaim to you about the Word of Life so that you may be united with us in the same faith. Life has appeared, it is revealed. This we proclaim to you so that you may have fellowship with us. Fellowship with us is fellowship with the Father and the Son. . . .

Where the Kingdom of God, the rule of Christ, is being proclaimed, things start happening. That is why John the Baptist was challenged: Why are you asking? Look at what is happening, listen to what is being said, and accept it. This is what is happening here: The blind see, the lame walk, lepers are cleansed, the deaf hear, the dead are raised. (Matt. 11:5)

Jesus is saying that if only you could believe what is actually happening, Christ would be revealed to you and your questions about God's Kingdom would be answered. That is what faith means. And because John the Baptist was not yet able to grasp this faith fully, Jesus told His disciples, "I tell you, there is none greater than John the Baptist among all the sons of women; yet he who is least in the Kingdom of Heaven is greater than he." (Matt. 11:11) The least in the Kingdom of God, the simplest in the Church, understand what is happening in faith. . . .

The apostles went out to tell people: Now the word of the prophets is coming true. Now it is coming—you can see it happening! Part of what was happening in Jerusalem was that Church community was being established. The Kingdom of God was drawing near—healing given through faith witnessed to that.

When the story of the apostles was written down, it was called The Acts of the Apostles because it described what the apostles did and what happened through them. It is an account of the same miraculous powers, the same deeds and events, that took place in the life of Jesus. Here too the decisive thing was the proclamation of God's Kingdom; and because the Kingdom of God came near, many signs and wonders took place.

Worship meeting, Alm Bruderhof, June 24, 1935

THE NEW ORDER
FLESHED OUT

Rhön Bruderhof Children's House, Harvest festival, 1932

The Church

THE NEED TO GATHER

The human race finds itself in such boundless misery because it has fallen into a state of hostility. It is split apart, lacerated. This cleft shows the disastrous degree to which coldness of heart and hostility has advanced in a divided humankind.

It was not always like that. The hour of humankind's birth was a time when people lived in peace with God and one another. There is simply no doubt that the cradle of humanity was Paradise. (Gen. 2:8–15)

What is Paradise? Paradise is peace. When all powers work together in one spirit, in unbroken harmony, that is the secret of peace. Peace is like a prism that gathers all the colors of the spectrum in the pure white light of the sun and refracts them as the resplendent hues of the rainbow. In this peace all powers and gifts are used to serve God. That is the peace humanity knew at its very beginning.

The Book of Genesis tells us that the man's task was to till and preserve the land, to name all creatures, and to be master over the animals. (Gen. 2:15, 19; 1:26–28) Humankind has not made any progress; in fact, the task set in Paradise is still not done. Yet from the outset humanity was given the task

47

to live in harmony and peace, in community of work, in creative fellowship.

Worship meeting, Rhön Bruderhof, Sept. 4, 1933

Everywhere the world is going to pieces. It is crumbling and rotting away. It is going through a process of disintegration. It is dying. And in these fearsome times, through the Holy Spirit Christ places the City-Church with its unconditional unity right into the world. (John 17:11, 23; Matt. 5:14) The only help for the world is to have a place of gathering, to have people whose will, undivided and free of doubt, is bent on gathering with others in unity.

Members' meeting, Rhön Bruderhof, Nov. 3, 1932

Paul the Apostle says that all nations of the earth shall be gathered in this Church, that the fences and walls between races, nations, classes, ranks, and individuals shall be broken down. (Col. 3:11) Not only shall the entire world be conquered for God, but the Church shall reveal a life of complete unity in the midst of it.

Members' meeting, Rhön Bruderhof, July 1, 1934

This is a time when the whole world is in extreme danger. It is urgent therefore that we decide to accept the gift God offers us: life in the communal Church, a life of unity.

Letter, Jan. 1933

We are not simply a society for colonizing, for forming new settlements or villages (as if there weren't enough villages already) where people live as close together and yet as far apart as anywhere else. Nor is it our aim to create a community of the human race or to bring people together for communal living just as they are.

If we wished to form a community based on mutual regard, each one of us could have stayed where he or she was. The people here are neither better nor worse than anywhere else. There would have been no need to come to the Bruderhof if we were seeking nothing but mutual human relationships in community. We could have found that anywhere. But it would have been a complete failure. All attempts based on the present state of humanity will be unsuccessful. Right from the beginning they are doomed to go bankrupt.

Rhön Bruderhof, Oct. 8, 1933

HOW WAS THE CHURCH ESTABLISHED?

No one person or group of people could have brought about the first Church community. No heights of oratory, no burning enthusiasm, could have awakened for Christ the thousands who were moved at the time, or produced the united life of the early Church. The friends of Jesus knew this very well. Had not the Risen One Himself commanded them to wait in Jerusalem for the fulfillment of the great promise? (Luke 24:49) John had baptized in water all those who listened to him. But the first Church was to be submerged in and filled with the holy wind of Christ's Spirit. (Acts 2:1–2)

"Das Geheimnis der Urgemeinde," Das neue Werk, *Aug. 1920*

The apostles were instructed to remain in Jerusalem until they were clothed with power from on high. That was the founding of the Church, which in turn was possible only through the fact of the resurrection. For what was the first thing the apostles proclaimed? "This one pure One, whom you have killed, has been awakened by God!" (Acts 2:22–24)

Rhön Bruderhof, 1933

At Pentecost the apostles of Jesus were suddenly able to feel so completely with other people that their hearers could take their words to heart, for these words echoed their mother tongue and their true calling. The crowd was moved by the same Spirit that spoke through the leaders; the listeners had the same overpowering experience as the speakers. (Acts 2:4–11)

It was neither hypnosis nor human persuasiveness. People allowed God to work in them; they were overpowered and filled by His Spirit. At that moment the only true collective soul took on shape and form; the organic unity of the mysterious Body of Christ, the Church community, was born. . . .

The crowds that were gathered from different nations for Pentecost cried out with one voice, "We hear them telling in our own tongues the mighty works of God!" (Acts 2:11) The great works of God were what counted, and nothing else. Pentecost was God's way of bringing about His future reign. Pentecost was His message of righteousness to all nations, a powerful demonstration of God's deeds for the whole of humankind and for each individual. . . .

When the murderers of Jesus stood in the presence of the living Christ, they were confronted with absolute truthfulness. Then they felt the need for forgiveness of their sins. They experienced the inner poverty that could be satisfied only through the gift of the Holy Spirit. The first response to this overwhelming inflow of the Spirit was the question that surged from people's hearts: "What shall we do?" (Acts 2:37)

As a result, there came about a complete transformation

of people's inner being, a reshaping of their lives. It was in fact the very change of heart and conduct that John the Baptist had proclaimed as the first requirement for the great revolution to come, the turning upside down of everything. We cannot separate personal rebirth from this total transformation in Christ.

"Das Geheimnis der Urgemeinde," Das neue Werk, *Aug. 1920*

When we speak of community, we mean community under the rulership of God, in keeping with the prophecies about God's Kingdom.

What is the Kingdom of God? It is community in God, community in God's justice, that is, justice in the sight of God, the social justice that is part of brotherly community. Love God! Love your neighbor! (Matt. 22:37–40) That is what justice means. Love God in such a way that you become one with Him. Love your neighbor in such a way that you become one with him. Jesus prays that the world may be able to tell who He is and what love is by looking at His disciples. That can only be if there is perfect unity among them. In the unity of the communal Church and the Kingdom, justice, peace, and joy meet and flow together.

This unity is what Jesus died for and rose for. His words, His deeds, His life were all for the sake of unity. And so this unity in the Spirit was there the moment the Holy Spirit was poured out at Pentecost. That is how the early Christians became one. They were united in the teaching of the apostles. They knew that the Holy Spirit was given both to the apostles and to them. So between them and the apostles there was complete unity in the understanding of the truth.

If we are united with that same Spirit by whom God was revealed, we are completely one with the apostolic Church and its witness, with the writings of the apostles and prophets.

That is our attitude to the Bible: The Bible witnesses to the Spirit of God's unity.

Meeting with guests, Rhön Bruderhof, Nov. 6, 1935

We oppose outright the present order of society. We represent a different order, that of the communal Church as it was in Jerusalem after the Holy Spirit was poured out. The multitude of believers became one heart and one soul. On the social level, their oneness was visible in their perfect brotherliness. On the economic level it meant that they gave up all private property and lived in complete community of goods, free from any compulsion. And so we are called to represent the same in the world today, which quite naturally will bring us into conflicts. We cannot put this burden on anybody unless he or she prizes the greatness of God's Kingdom above everything else and feels inwardly certain that there is no other way to go.

Members' meeting, Rhön Bruderhof, Mar. 26, 1933

We celebrate the outpouring of the Holy Spirit and the beginning of full community because it meant that Paradise was given back in the midst of an unpeaceful, hostile environment. Jesus had begun this spiritual battle against the injustice of mammon, against impurity in human relationships, and against killing and war. The Church of Jesus Christ is set right into this world to be a place where peace, joy, and justice abide, a place of love and unity. That is the Church's calling. And that is why the Apostle says the Kingdom of God does not consist in abstaining from this or that kind of food, but in justice and peace and joy in the Holy Spirit. (Rom. 14:17) This is what actually happened in Jerusalem! It had already happened in Jesus' time in a very small circle among the Twelve. In Je-

rusalem it happened among thousands of people with a force
that radiated into the entire accessible world of that day.

And in the following centuries this mission was never lost.
Its light shone in Asia Minor; it penetrated as far as southern
France, to the southwestern part of the Alps, to North Africa,
to the plateaus of northern Italy, along the Rhine, as far north
as Holland and England, and to the eastern Alps, Moravia,
and Bohemia. This community of total sharing shone its rays
into every century. Again and again this sacred spark was
fanned to a holy flame. It was never extinguished, for the Holy
Spirit will not retreat from the earth until the whole creation
celebrates the victory of God's Kingdom, and peace, justice,
and joy in love and unity reign in all the world.

Worship meeting, Rhön Bruderhof, Sept. 4, 1933

The only way the world will recognize the mission of Jesus is by the unity of His Church. But this unity of the Church
must be translated into total community. Jesus spoke of the
absolute unity between His Father and Himself. And His
prayer for us is that we be just as united. (John 17:21–22) Can
there still be mine and thine between us? No. What is mine is
thine, and what is thine is mine. In the Spirit of the Church
everything we have belongs to all. First and foremost we have
community in the innermost values of the common life. But if
we share the treasures of the Spirit, which are the greater
ones, how can we refuse to share the lesser things?

Meeting with guests, Rhön Bruderhof, Aug. 15, 1934

AUTHORITY FOR MISSION

For mission you must have authorization and a power sta-
tion where you can receive inner strength and support, a central place where you will find the help and correction you

need. And that place is the Church community. Ultimately, not the Church here on earth, but the Church that is above, the Jerusalem above that is mother of us all. This highest City of God sends its light down to the little bands united in faith on this earth. The more deeply they are united, the more authority they receive.

Meeting with guests, Rhön Bruderhof, Dec. 30, 1934

It is a great thing if we can go out and tell people about God's Kingdom. But it is a much greater thing if an historical reality is presented to the world, a witness to the truth of the Gospel to be unforgettably branded into the records of history. It means much more than our limited attempts to convert individuals, if we are called to participate in making history by representing with our lives the way of love and peace and justice in the midst of a hostile, untruthful, unjust world that is bristling with weapons—if we are called to live out this witness, unperturbed and unswayed, while around us the nations rage. That is the Church's true calling.

Worship meeting, Rhön Bruderhof, Nov.12, 1933

GOD'S EMBASSY

In view of the widespread evil in the world, the Church community acknowledges that the use of government force is unavoidable. But what is entrusted to the Church is something completely different.

Each kingdom or nation maintains an embassy in Paris, Petersburg, Berlin, Rome, and other capitals. The embassy building is sacrosanct territory, where no one is subject to the laws of the country surrounding the embassy; in the embassy building only the laws of its own country are in effect.

It is just the same with the Church. Jesus Christ sends His Church, led by the Holy Spirit, to be His embassy. Here the final law is that of the final Kingdom. Therefore the Church community should not unthinkingly submit to the laws of today's governments. It should honor them, but it should not be bound to them in slavish obedience. (Acts 5:27–29)

Rhön Bruderhof, May 31, 1934
(See also ch. "Attitude to Government")

In the twentieth century this is as true as ever: The way is narrow, and those who find it are few. (Matt. 7:14) But it is not only a way. It is not only a narrow mountain path. It is at the same time a city on a hill that can be seen all around. Because it is visible to all, it is significant for all, even for those who do not want to go the way, who have no desire to enter the city. They see the possibility, and their attention is drawn to the coming Kingdom. And they will think, if God's love came down upon us all in this way, then we would all live together in peace, unity, and justice. (Matt. 5:14–16)

That is the service we must do for the world. It is the practical outcome of following Jesus.

Meeting with guests, Alm Bruderhof, Aug. 22, 1934

God is patient with humankind. He interposed the Church so that, while this world age lasts, individual people might be called out, so that in the midst of this world a living monument to His patience might be erected to represent the fellowship of the Cross. The fellowship of His blood, the fellowship of the Cross, shows us what it means to die with Him. And that can only be shown in the lowly Church, in the interim between the Cross of Christ and the second coming of Christ.

Meeting with guests, Rhön Bruderhof, July 1, 1934

Unity and the Holy Spirit

The Church community is to be a city on a hill, with light from its windows shining out over the land, so that all who see it will realize: There is a united city, a united Church! (Matt. 5:14) This is the call of Jesus in our time, that communal Churches are brought into being, whose light of perfect unity, of justice, peace, and joy in the Holy Spirit, shines out into the world.

Meeting with guests, Rhön Bruderhof, Aug. 12, 1935

UNANIMITY IS POSSIBLE

We are not optimistic about world politics. We do have faith that the Church can give witness to unity and that this witness is the best service we can do for the world. Full community, full agreement, is possible! It is possible through faith in God, in Christ, and in the Holy Spirit. This is what our life is about.

Meeting with guests, Alm Bruderhof, July 25, 1935

Unimpaired unanimity is indispensable for anything the community undertakes, building a house or whatever it may be. This unanimity is only possible because of our faith that God uses His Spirit to say the same to each individual. Mutual persuasion does not do it. God does it, speaking to us through the Holy Spirit. This Spirit not only assures us of our salvation—that He has accepted us—but His speaking to us also makes us certain even in the so-called "trifles" or small matters. He prompts us also in making decisions such as buying a meadow, or whatever it may be. Unanimity is the first sign.

The second sign is the work itself. People normally work to support their families, from a healthy, natural instinct. But more often than not their only reason for holding a particular job is to earn a living. The rest of their life has no connection with their work. We fight against that. Just as there should be concord between people, so there should be harmony between the work a person does and his or her inner calling. (Col. 3:17, 23) All strength and all gifts must be devoted to this work, in the Spirit of the Church.

Rhön Bruderhof, 1929

COMMUNITY, NOT UNIFORMITY

Only if we have willing, sincere, and open hearts will we find unanimity in our convictions. We have never found it disturbing when people have come to us representing convictions that differ from ours. On the contrary, that is more fruitful than if we had no chance to hear opposing ideas. We believe that a free exchange of ideas can help people to recognize the truth, thanks to a Spirit that does not originate with us human beings. Then, no matter how diverse our opinions may have been, through the ultimate truth we will all be united. Each one will bring from the storehouse of his earlier convictions those elements that are true, and he will find these again. And the more varied our different backgrounds are, the richer the fruits of this diversity will be. A united conviction can never be produced by forcing anyone to comply. Only the Holy

Spirit with His power of inner persuasion leads people from freedom of opinions to true unity.

Mealtime at the Rhön Bruderhof, May 20, 1933

It is a remarkable thing when people decide something unanimously. It is the opposite of making a majority decision. Unanimity means that nobody disagrees with it or opposes it, not even in secret. (1 Cor. 1:10)

Rhön Bruderhof, 1929

When people believe in unity, it creates a very strong bond. It is a deplorable fact that some who call themselves Christians are so very disunited, not only in the various world Churches but also among those who try to be real Christians. And it is no help at all to decide to be silent about those subjects people don't see eye to eye on. Many a one feels: Today is the day for worship, the day to go to church, to serve God; tomorrow I will be at my job and lead my personal and family life. How will such a person ever find unity and harmony within, let alone with others?

There is nothing that surpasses perfect unity. That is God's mystery—joy and unity in His creative Spirit. So the question now is: Do we really believe in God? Do we really believe that He will triumph in His intent to bring about unity? Do we believe that it will happen here and now, provided we want nothing but God and His way?

Rhön Bruderhof, Mar. 19, 1933

NOT A HUMAN BOND

Because the flame from the other world really does come to us, we can say with assurance that we are not satisfied with finding an intellectual unanimity. It is not enough to set a common goal and use all our will power to reach it; nor is it enough to vibrate together in an emotional experience. We know that something quite different has to come over us that will lift us out of this purely human level.

Rhön Bruderhof, Mar. 18, 1932

Just as the sun's rays constantly shine upon our earth, just as lightning from the clouds brings down light and fire, so too an element has to burst into our midst that does not come from us. It will not come from our noblest feelings or from what is holiest within us. It has to be something that overwhelms us, something we cannot give to each other. We witness to the fact that this overpowering element makes us conscious of our unity and brings us complete unison of thought, will, and feeling. (Eph. 3:14–19)

Worship meeting, Rhön Bruderhof, Mar. 19, 1933

One may ask how the Church, the Church of the heavenly realm, works in the lives of people here on earth. There is but one answer faith can give, namely, that through the Holy Spirit the Church of Jesus Christ comes down to the earth; the Holy Spirit is at work in the Church continually in just the same way as at Jerusalem when the Spirit was first poured out on all flesh. Wherever the Church comes down in the reality of the Holy Spirit, its life has a sociological impact that is no different from what happened at Pentecost in Jerusalem.

Rhön Bruderhof, Mar. 1, 1933

THE HOLY SPIRIT GATHERS

God, who created all things and without whom nothing has come into being, sent His Holy Spirit upon the earth and to all people. This Spirit wants to gather all, to bring them together. Jesus was placed in the world by this Spirit to live among people, and He in turn testified to the gathering power of the Holy Spirit, saying, "How often would I have gathered your children; but you would not let me." (Matt. 23:37) But He was taken away from those who did not want to let themselves be gathered. He was killed by the spirit that scatters, by the power that drives apart. (Matt. 12:30)

Yet He, the Living One, returned to His own. "Receive the Holy Spirit! As the Father has sent me, even so I send you." (John 20:21–22) "What you gather on earth will be gathered; what you loose will be loosed; and what you bind will be bound." (Matt. 18:18) From that moment on, all those whose hearts were gripped by this Spirit felt the need to be together. Under the stress of their sorrow they stayed together and waited in holy expectation. Those were long weeks of waiting. This tense expectancy must always be there before a complete uniting can be given. Unity is not accomplished by a meeting of minds, by a coalition of individual human spirits. It is found exclusively through the coming down and breaking in of that Spirit which is not a human spirit.

Members' meeting, Rhön Bruderhof, Nov. 3, 1932

We ask the Holy Spirit that the Church of light and of love may shine down on us from all the centuries, from all Eternity, and that we may be completely united with it. We ask that the Spirit of the Church may be poured out over us with all its powers, setting us on fire. We ask that we in our humble place may be used wherever the Spirit wants us, not where we want to be. We do not want to gird ourselves but long to be used wherever God, who rules over the history of all worlds, wants to use us. We ask to be led in such a way that the fire He has kindled in us may fulfill His task.

Worship meeting, Rhön Bruderhof, June 3, 1933

BEYOND THE PERSONAL

Personal piety has become widespread, but unfortunately it is confined to what could be called purely religious experience, which cannot stand before God. Many of these exclusively religious movements have arisen in recent years, confining themselves to preaching and personal confessions of faith, to a private experience of the Savior and a very limited personal sanctification.

However much we rejoice that people are awakened to a love for Jesus, that they experience forgiveness of sin in His death on the Cross, we must state that Christ's love and the meaning of His death on the Cross are not fully understood if they are restricted to the individual's subjective experience of salvation. It was to be foreseen years ago that the influence of modern theology would be disastrous.* True, it did show us something great: God is totally other than all our movements for personal salvation or social reform. Yet a one-sided emphasis on this otherness, which removes the living God to the distant Beyond, is bound to have the effect of minimizing or even suppressing social responsibility.

Worship meeting, Rhön Bruderhof, Nov. 21, 1934

It is truly Christian to proclaim the good news of the pardoned sinner, who is now able to lead a purified life so as to belong more and more to Christ. (Col. 1:28) The New Testament, in fact the whole Bible, speaks of it. That is why we are thankful that movements have sprung up again and again of people who long to be purified for God by Jesus their Savior. Such waves of inner revival keep recurring, and that is a great

---

*A reference to "dialectical theology."

grace. We are thankful that very many of us have experienced something of Christ in similar movements.

It is important to observe, however, that the purely personal approach does not bring satisfaction in the long run. A Christianity that concentrates only on the individual soul and its experience cannot endure for long.

Meeting with guests, Rhön Bruderhof, July 1, 1934

The revelation of the Holy Spirit does not stop at any boundary, least of all the boundary that divides the spiritual from the material. The Holy Spirit is a creative Spirit. He seeks the way from the heart of God right down into the material world. We believe it is the will of the Holy Spirit to bring about true community precisely in material things, including work with the elements of the earth. We believe that the unity of the Spirit is present in the so-called outward aspects of life just as much as in the innermost concerns of faith. Faith urges us to do the deeds of love. In other words, faith wants to use love to transform matter so that it can be fitted into God's Kingdom and His justice. The unity among us must extend to everyday things. And the more we are animated by the Spirit, the more we will surmount our practical problems.

Meeting with guests, Alm Bruderhof, July 25, 1935

Our reverence for the reality of the Holy Spirit must become so great that our trivial personal concerns, including our state of health and our emotional needs, will be consumed as in a mighty flame.

When the great hour comes, will there be a generation worthy of it? As far as humankind is concerned, only one thing is worthy of the greatness of God's Kingdom: the readiness to die. But unless we prove our readiness in the trivialities of daily life, we shall not be able to muster up courage in the critical hour of history. In our communal life we need to overcome completely all our petty attitudes and feelings, to give up all personal ways of reacting to things, that is, fear, worry, inner uncertainty—in short, unbelief. Instead, we need faith, a faith as small as a tiny seed but with the same potential to grow. (Luke 17:6) This is what we need, neither more nor less.

Through Christ and His Holy Spirit, this faith is at work in our midst. We have felt it, but we have not lived accordingly. If the Holy Spirit had to withdraw from us because we have grieved Him and driven Him away, have not held Him in reverence but thought little of Him, valuing our own affairs higher, then all we can do is ask, "Send Thy judgment upon us, and in Thy infinite mercy spare nothing!" And then this judgment in mercy, this mercy in judgment, will release us from ourselves and prepare us at last for mission, making us ready for God to use.

Rhön Bruderhof, Aug. 26, 1928

If we live according to our old nature, we cannot represent anything good, even if we base it on the Bible. But in the new creation, in Christ, in His Spirit, wherever His Spirit is present without being distorted or caricatured, indestructible community has arisen among people. Let him grasp it who can! The truth of the Bible is not intellectual or logical truth. It is beyond logic. It is given only to those who believe. (1 Cor. 2:12–13)

So we are faced with quite practical questions: Do we believe that the Holy Spirit will be increasingly poured out over the Church? Do we believe that Jesus comes into our midst, that He opens His heart to us so that we may live as He did and have an influence in society as He did? Do we dare to carry out the task as His Church in His coming Kingdom, to be a corrective within society through the grace of the indwelling Christ? Do we dare to live a life of love in the midst of the world, giving up all privilege and even the right to our possessions and our own bodies? Are we ready, completely defenseless, to follow Jesus?

Public lecture, Nov. 28, 1922

Community

COMMUNITY OF GOODS GROWS OUT OF LOVE

Jesus showed us what it means to love—that love knows no bounds and stops before no barriers. Nothing can stop love, even if circumstances seem to block the way. Love had, and has, faith for everything. (1 Cor. 13:7–8) So Jesus, prompted always by love, did not let property or possessions stop Him. When He came to know and love a young man who owned many possessions, Jesus looked straight into his heart and said, "You still lack one thing: Sell all your goods, give the money to the poor, and come, go with me." (Mark 10:21)

Bible study session, 1919

The first Church in Jerusalem distributed all their goods straightaway. As soon as Christ's Spirit was poured out over them, nobody could hold on to property any longer. Love compelled them to lay everything at the apostles' feet. With the help of the deacons the apostles distributed everything. (Acts 6:2–6) Christ's love makes us want to give up our possessions and live in community of goods. (Acts 4:32–37) That strikes at the root of our selfishness.

Meeting with guests, Rhön Bruderhof, May 1935

To give away your cloak as well when only your coat is asked for is truly in keeping with love. But to put in a second hour of work when one hour is asked for means much more. (Matt. 5:38–42) The fight against private property must be preceded by something deeper: the killing of selfishness, self-love, self-will, and self-importance.

Mennonitische Blätter, Apr. 1929

Religion and devout feelings are useless unless they are expressed in action and in truth, that is, in real community. (1 John 3:17–18) Jesus says, Love God! And the other command is exactly the same: Love your neighbor! There is no true love to God if it is not a true love to our fellow human being, and vice versa. (Matt. 22:36–39)

This has been our experience: Community is possible through the Spirit that comes to us from God. It is when this Spirit fills us that there is true love for our neighbor and full community among us.

Mealtime at the Rhön Bruderhof, Sept. 1935

PEOPLE CANNOT BUILD COMMUNITY

It is certainly true that God works in people, in all men and women. But as soon as this truth is exaggerated to the point where we believe solely in ourselves and other human beings, we are on the wrong track. We must believe in God in such a way that not the individual but God is in the center, and that individuals join with each other in submitting to His will. God's will can then work in us and through us, and we ourselves become so transparent—like a window—that our own human life no longer matters at all: God's working is all that is seen. I do not believe community can come into being in any other way. No matter how humble, dedicated, and un-assuming a person may be, he cannot build community in his own strength. (2 Cor. 12:9)

Rhön Bruderhof, July 31, 1933

Our faith in God is not the product of our wishful think-ing; the basis of our communal life is God and God alone. But we cannot say we have acquired this basis and now we own re-ligion as one owns property. What we have must be given to us new each day. It is a dreadful thought, but we have to face it: We can lose it any day. All we can say is that we are placed on this foundation by God's grace. Our faith does not result from our natural abilities; the Holy Spirit has to lead us there.

Rhön Bruderhof, July 24, 1933

We have nothing. If we ever thought we had community, we have now seen that we do not have it. And it is good for us to have seen that. Community exists exclusively in Christ and His life-giving Spirit. If we forget Him and are left without His influence, if we forfeit His working among us, it is all over with our community. (John 15:5)

Members' meeting, Rhön Bruderhof, Nov. 2, 1935

CAN THE INVISIBLE CHURCH BECOME VISIBLE?

The invisible Church must become visible. For this to happen, community of goods and work and a common table are needed. The Church of Christ is active everywhere, though invisible, wherever people are gripped by Christ's Spirit. A life in full community, though, makes visible this invisible unity, not only in religious practices but in the whole of life.

Meeting with guests, Rhön Bruderhof, Aug. 14, 1935

The stream of unity flows from the fountainhead of the Spirit into all areas: first into the heart-to-heart relationships among the members and then into the things around us. Out of community in the Spirit grows community of education and of work, and that naturally means community of goods without any private property, because the mainspring of our life is love. Love is joy in one another. This joy, welling up from the fountain of unity, enables us to surrender everything. Giving up a sum of money means nothing compared with surrendering all our strength. (Luke 9:23–24) Wealth stems from the resources of the earth and from human labor. We share both earth's resources and our working strength. But with all that, we do not want to live in collective egotism just to support ourselves as a community. Rather, we have to make this possibility known: people can live in community! We bear witness to this reality: people are living in community! We bear witness to the wellspring of this reality: the future Kingdom of God.

Mealtime at the Alm Bruderhof, Sept. 24, 1934

Touchiness, opinionatedness, self-love, self-centeredness —all these are obstacles. It is a deadly poison to have a higher opinion of oneself than of others. (Phil. 2:3) Anyone who still has that attitude is basically incapable of community. He will be incapable of partaking in the unity we want to live for. This is a very important point. To think of others and their situation and to look for the best in them will help us not to see ourselves in a better light than others. It is easy to see the shortcomings of others out of all proportion and forget that we ourselves are weak human beings. We should not always be trying to correct other people's mistakes. We have to reconcile ourselves to human imperfection.

Rhön Bruderhof, Aug. 9, 1933

IS COMMUNITY GOD'S WILL?

A guest asked: Do you mean to say that the Bruderhof is God's will?

Eberhard: Not the Bruderhof, but total community. What we have recognized as being important is the life Jesus lived with His disciples and the life of the first Church in Jerusalem. We see the prophetic Old Testament likewise as a Word from God that we should live together in Church community (Ps. 133), in peace and justice and joy, as the Apostle Paul puts it. (Rom. 14:17) Our whole life is meant only humbly to suggest the way.

Meeting with guests, Rhön Bruderhof, Aug. 22, 1935

We believe in God's mercy for everyone. For this reason we feel no need to make all humankind members of the Bruderhof, although we are glad about each one who enters into community with us. We don't think that anyone who doesn't come to us is lost, but we want to live this way to the end of our lives because we believe that this is our calling for the sake of all humankind. The fulfillment of this calling does not depend on how many want to join us in community. It simply means living together in such a way that our life reveals God's love and unity in a positive, concrete way. Again and again, and rightly, the words of the Bible, "God is love," are underlined; we are deeply convinced that they are true. We can also turn this around and say, "Wherever there is true love, God is there." (1 John 4:8, 11–12)

So it is clear to us that this true love means unity and community, mutual help and service, renunciation of anything of our own, and joy in one another! Then we are united in love and can say, "God is unity, and he who remains in this unity remains in God and God in him." (1 John 4:16)

Meeting with novices and guests, Rhön Bruderhof, Jan. 1935

IS COMMUNITY ESCAPE?

Our community life first came into being because of the widespread need around us. The reason we left the big cities was not to withdraw from the world. And in moving to this place on a mountain (so very isolated at first sight) we had no intention of evading our responsibility to society. Rather, we felt that by concentrating our forces we might best be able to influence society at large. And still today our first and foremost concern is that our communal life may have an effect on the world around us. (John 17:20–23)

Meeting with guests, Rhön Bruderhof, Oct. 6, 1932

We are always surprised when people say that we no longer live in the world because we live in a Bruderhof or any other community. We live in the midst of the world the same as anyone else. We are not ghosts, but people of flesh and blood right here on earth, and we too have to ask for protection from evil in the world, otherwise we are lost. (John 17:15–16) This mistake comes from a spiritualization of Jesus' words that is not the Spirit of Jesus. It transforms the realism of the Bible into the twilight of unclarity.

Rhön Bruderhof, Jan. 13, 1933

We are told to be on the lookout not for our own advantage but for that of our fellows. (1 Cor. 10:24) How can this be done? Only in a community life of complete dedication where all property is held in common. It goes without saying that communal property must never lead to collective egotism. It is not meant to be a common enterprise for the benefit of its members, nor a partnership for the profit of its partners. Instead, all common property must be dedicated to a service that benefits all, to the community of all humankind in God's future Kingdom, to the positive Christian faith that turns toward the whole of humanity.

Meeting with guests, Rhön Bruderhof, Aug. 14, 1935

THE POWER OF MONEY

The fall consisted in this: Human beings took as their possession not what God gave them, but what the Devil gave. This is the root of sin—taking possession of property. The covetous will, wanting to have something for one's own, is the very substance of evil. That is what the story of the apple is all about (though the Bible does not speak of an apple). But humankind rejected what God had given them, that is, community with God. They despised what God had given them. They appropriated something that God had not given them. That is why mammon is the Devil. (Matt. 6:24ff)*

Meeting with guests, Rhön Bruderhof, May 1935

Evil is not just a concept; it is a reality. Death is evil. Anything that leads to death, destruction, separation, mistrust, and

---

*"Mammon" is derived from the Aramaic word *mamona*, probably meaning riches or profit; sometimes translated in Matt. 6:24 as money.

division is evil. Prostitution is evil and therefore has devastating effects.

Evil is not merely the absence of good, a standing apart from God's life. It is a mistake to think that evil is simply a negation of good, a mere deficit. Death is a power, mammon is a power. Money is a personification of Satan; it is the Devil personified. The same is true of murder and impurity. There is a tremendous power behind all these things. (John 8:44) If money were nothing but a medium of exchange for goods and work, it would not be evil. But it is not true to say money is only a medium of exchange; it is a means to power. This is what is devilish about it: It is a means to power over people's lives. Within a community there is no need for money. In a really communal life money is totally superfluous; in fact it is the antithesis of community.

Meeting with guests, Rhön Bruderhof, Oct. 22, 1935

At the beginning in Sannerz, there were immature moments when our little community considered having pocket money [for private spending]. Today we know that keeping any kind of money separate from the communal purse sounds the death knell of brotherly community.

1930

Jesus opened up the struggle against property. He Himself had left all that was His own; He had abandoned all privileges and given up all He possessed in order to go the way of love and sacrifice. (Matt. 8:20)

He was our example because He wanted no property. From manger to Cross, He was the poorest. Gather no treasure for yourselves, gather no property; instead, store up something different for yourselves, that is, the love of your fellows. Let go of money, the perishable wealth, and instead take hold of imperishable wealth; then you will be rich. (Matt. 6:19–20)

Public meeting near the Rhön Bruderhof, Oct. 1931

Now something new is being demanded of you. You are expected to administer faithfully this wicked offspring of god-forsaken matter, namely money, so that you can do something for God's Kingdom even with this thing that is alien to you. That means of course that money should be used immediately. If you give it away it will be essential to give it where it is needed, not to increase a rich man's bank account. It must be used to produce new assets that are no longer tainted with mammon, that are no longer alien to the Spirit—assets that will pass the test of Eternity. . . .

When people come to the realization of personal sin, an icy shock passes through them. They cannot imagine how through Christ they could be united with the heart of the Father and with the Church. And just because it is such a great shock, something so unbelievable, this is the point where faith begins.

It is exactly the same in material matters. When these things give us the worst fright and we are utterly helpless, unable to imagine how a Spirit beyond the earth can master earthly things like these, just then faith begins. Faith is the only way we are shown; we have no other. (Matt. 6:24–34) And this faith is faithfulness and trust. The secret of faith in this area lies in our approach to questions of income and expenditure, to matters concerning farm, workshop, building, and office: We must allow the Holy Spirit to show us the way. We need to keep a wholesome awareness of our financial situation so that we can be deeply shaken by what God does.

Worship meeting, Rhön Bruderhof, June 21, 1934

COMMUNITY IS WORK

We believe in a Christianity that does something. Daily work with others is the best and quickest way to find out whether we are willing to live in community on the basis of real love and faith. Work is the crucial test that shows whether our faith is genuine.

Alm Bruderhof leaflet, May 1934

Faith put into practice in community life is the secret that brings a close relationship between matters of faith and work. (Col. 3:23–24) Most people are unable to find a relationship between these two areas. Even for those who can testify to genuine Christian experiences, these two areas of life are separate; they go in opposite directions.

People may live their inner life in the holiest things and try to hold on to them while at the same time the practical aspects of their life on this earth move further and further away from the Holy Spirit. We are subject to the same danger; we aren't the slightest bit different from other people. In our communal Church life, however, we have been given a glimpse of the mystery that connects these two areas of life in a way we never knew before. The connection is a deep one, based on the apostolic faith: We believe in the Maker of the first creation just as much as we believe in the One who redeems us for His new creation, and we believe in the Spirit who shows us the way to it.

Worship meeting, Rhön Bruderhof, June 21, 1934

Prayer must never supplant work in God's Kingdom and in His Church. We pray for God's will to be done on earth, for His nature to be revealed in deeds, for His rule to bring unity, justice, and love. If we are serious in our request, our life will mean hard work. Faith without action is dead. (James 2:17) Prayer without work is hypocrisy. Unless we live according to God's Kingdom, we make the Lord's Prayer a lie. The Lord's Prayer should put us into the framework in which what we ask for actually happens, becomes part of history. For us the Bruderhof with its communal life is the God-appointed place where we can give our whole working strength so that He is honored, His will is done, and His Kingdom comes. Unless love among brothers and sisters results in work and action, the tree of our life will wither and come under judgment.

1929; English translation: Prayer Life, *pp. 46–47*

People are happiest when they can use their strength in healthy productivity and actually see the results of their work. Certainly, if they are to be happy in their work, they have to find the job they are fitted for, the job they enjoy because it comes naturally to them.

It is commonly argued that this is a utopia and that no one would do menial tasks unless compelled; but this reasoning is based on the false premise of present-day humanity in its moral decline. Nowadays most people lack the spirit of love that makes the lowliest practical job a joy and delight. The difference between respectable and degrading work disappears when we have to nurse or look after someone we love. Love removes that difference and makes anything we do for the beloved person an honor.

It is an unhealthy symptom of our civilization that many think of physical work as an inferior kind of activity, something nobody enjoys. But we human beings are in fact not made to concern ourselves exclusively with spiritual or intellectual matters. Healthy people have an urge to do simple physical work on the land; they enjoy sun and light, mountains and woods, plants and animals, farm and garden. Pleasure in physical activity is natural and brings joy in life, in God and His creation.

"Jesus und der Zukunftsstaat,"
unpublished article, 1919

COMING TOGETHER

No community that exists for its own sake can survive. (John 15:4) It would be a sect, something cut off. It would lose the way by becoming isolated, no matter how much it practiced community.

Rhön Bruderhof, 1929

We had searched the ages and the nations and continents thoroughly and systematically for people who lived together in total community, in perfect love and absolute peace, in complete freedom of the Spirit and full unity. We had searched for traveling companions, for proved and tested groups of pilgrims on the same way. We were never in the least interested in founding our own movement or maintaining our own enterprise. We never cared the least to assert our so-called independence or to win the reputation of having a lifework of our own. Away with anything of our own! All that mattered to us was that our call was clear, our freedom pure, and our unity real. That alone had to be kept alive and deepened. So we looked out for men and women, for individuals and groups, who might be following this call to freedom, purity, and unity better than we had been able to do and who might thus be an example to us.

And we did in fact encounter several community attempts, some large and some smaller groups, some old and some of recent origin. How much we rejoiced at every drop of life that flowed into the greater stream of life, at every tiny living organism that showed signs of a greater unity! Many little communal groups in our own and neighboring countries were young and frail in their origins; but we also found several movements that had been living in full vigor for two, three, or even four centuries in complete community in a freeing and uniting spirit—and still are living today!

Meeting with guests, Rhön Bruderhof, Sept. 9, 1935

Repentance and Baptism

WHAT IS SIN?

Humanity's measureless estrangement from God is the root cause of their sinking deeper and deeper into depravity, physically as well as otherwise. (Rom. 1:18–32) To live means to shed everything that is death-bound. We are hopelessly sick in our sin and will really die unless we are freed from sin and evil. (Rom. 6:20–23) Hatred and murder, lying, cowardice, dishonesty, impurity, and degeneration in the sensual area are life-destroyers. Slowly but surely they smother the last flicker of real life in us, while dazzling us with the illusion of intense vitality.

"Jesus und der Zukunftsstaat,"
unpublished article, 1919

Is all sin a form of sickness? If we say it is, we run the risk of softening the fact that we are responsible. That is extremely dangerous. Humanity is subject to death, and that is sickness; but Scripture shows us that the poisonous element in death is sin and that, if we were not in bondage to sin, we would not die. (Rom. 5:12) And sin is our own doing. By sinning we dissolve our fellowship with God and join in an evil fellowship with forces hostile to God.

Sin creates a bond with poison. Sin destroys life. It severs community with God—the living relationship with God, who is the life-giving Spirit. Even though we know that sin is connected with the sickness which is death, we are responsible for our sin; it is our action, our will.

Members' meeting, Rhön Bruderhof, July 1933

It would be wrong to say yes to everything in life just as it is. We have to take a definite attitude to both the pleasures and the trials life has in store. Although even the worst evil may have a meaning in the course of history, yet anyone who is gripped by God has to take a stand against it. He or she must root the same evil out of his or her own life and endeavor to overcome it for all of humankind. Though this is a fighting attitude, it is a genuine affirmation of life. True life cannot include anything that leads to falsehood, disloyalty, untruthfulness, ill will, or letting money and other external things dominate us. That would be enslavement, a basic denial of life. Only when the Spirit takes hold of our lives can we take a truly positive attitude by affirming the greatest thing, love, and rejecting everything else.

Mealtime at the Rhön Bruderhof, Jan. 30, 1933

REPENTANCE

Repentance means that a man or a woman feels repelled and disgusted by his or her whole sinfulness and by each of his or her separate sins. They become utterly obnoxious. Repentance is the pain of being absolutely repelled by one's sins; it is the remorseful feeling that one would give one's life if only by doing so one could undo them; it is the pervasive sense of horror, of wanting to die rather than to go along with any of these things again even to the slightest degree. Repentance is remorse, a complete emotional break with the wrong life that was trying to put the individual with his or her demonic tendencies in the place of God.

Rhön Bruderhof, Sept. 22, 1935

To repent we must first of all recognize and admit fully the gravity of what we have done, its accursedness. We must see plainly that what we have done is destructive and murderous. Then the rest will come, step by step.

It is important not to speak about being freed in one area unless at the same time we are freed in all other areas. We should not think we are taking a firm stand in the political situation or claim to be radically free from social injustice unless we are free at the same time from lying and immorality. It is impossible to condemn and combat one while being soft and spineless in another.

Members' meeting, Rhön Bruderhof, July 1933

The rebirth Jesus spoke about to the man who came to Him at night means repentance. (John 3:1ff) And repentance means a thorough upheaval. In this rebirth we are exonerated from all our sins, we are redeemed because our sins are forgiven and overcome through Jesus, the Crucified and Risen One. The upheaval that comes with repentance begins by revolutionizing our moral life. Unless we give up all evil, there is no real change, no true repentance. As long as we commit sin, we are slaves of sin. If we are born of God, we will not sin.

Public lecture, Nov. 1917

FORGIVENESS FOLLOWS REPENTANCE

We confess that we are not and cannot be without sin. We remain in need of forgiveness, and therefore we must ask for forgiveness. Just as we need forgiveness for ourselves, we must forgive others. And Christ, who came from Heaven to help us on earth, will give us the strength for this.

This is the message we have to proclaim: We can be freed from our own flesh, our willfulness, and this will enable us to love others with such love that we can forgive them wholeheartedly their guilt toward us. Then our hearts will be renewed, and we will take a straightforward stand on justice, the justice of God's Kingdom.

Worship meeting, Rhön Bruderhof, Jan. 24, 1935

Jesus gave His Spirit, with full authority to represent His Kingdom, to the unity of the Church, that is, to the unity of the apostles. Their authority to loose and to bind—to forgive and leave unforgiven—makes it possible for people to be completely freed so that they can enter the Kingdom of God. No conscience can live without forgiveness of sins. No one can see the Kingdom of God without it. United in faith and in life, the Church of God is entrusted with the power to forgive sins, which is valid before all people's consciences; as its charge and prerogative for this day and age, it is given the life of Jesus and His future rule.

Inner Land, p. 170

Let us thank God for the forgiveness of sin. Without it we cannot stand before God for one day; without it we cannot live in community one day. Without forgiveness of sin there is no joy and no love, for only one who has been forgiven much loves much. (Luke 7:47) Let us thank God that the sacrament of forgiveness is alive among us. We pray for the power of the Holy Spirit to help us to forgive, every hour and every moment, whatever wrong has been done to us and whatever imperfections remain among us. We can only ask God to forgive our sins if we have forgiven all who have sinned against us. (Matt. 6:12)

Worship meeting, Rhön Bruderhof, July 31, 1933

BAPTISM

Baptism takes us into the death of Jesus, so that we may experience resurrection with Him—the central core of salvation. To be redeemed, then, this nature must go through death, so that through resurrection we become truly alive, so that the old nature is changed into the new creation. This is the belief we testify to in baptism, the faith that the Holy Spirit will be poured out over the person who is being baptized and that the love of God will take hold of his or her life. (Acts 2:38)

Worship meeting, Alm Bruderhof, June 2, 1935

We want to state clearly that it is completely against our way of life to press anyone to state his or her confession of faith in a set form of words. Far from it. Just because we really believe in God, in Christ, and in His Spirit, we cannot see any point in compelling people to express the same faith in the same way. What we confess to is so immeasurably superior to us human beings that there is no need to persuade others to profess the same. The fact that a person does not confess to God does not change God.

Meeting with novices and guests,
Rhön Bruderhof, Jan. 1935

We believe in God our Father because we have received His childlike Spirit. We acknowledge Him as Creator of heaven and earth. Therefore we cannot adore any of His creatures in the place of God, either in the world of spirits or in nature.

We have found Him in Jesus Christ, King of the coming Kingdom, the Christ who has become our Lord and Master, whose words we obey and according to whose Spirit we live. We know that this Christ is the selfsame historical Jesus who was born of the Virgin Mary and was executed by the Roman State at the hands of Pontius Pilate. We know that His ministry reached down into Hell and to the graves of the dead. And we know that He proclaimed His Gospel there and continues to proclaim it just as He proclaims it among the people now living on earth.

And we know that He who lay in the grave has truly arisen from the dead and has taken His place on the heavenly throne in the majesty of God's Kingdom. And we expect Him to come from there and judge all humankind on that day when the Book of Life is opened, when the Last Judgment shall come over everything that glorifies human beings, so that God alone rules in His Kingdom.

We believe in the Holy Spirit, who is truly holy because He is not stained with evil. He has no fellowship with evil but unites us in the unity of the one universal Church. We do not believe in a pantheism of combined good and evil.

Through the Holy Spirit we believe in the unity of the Church, in that Church where forgiveness of sins is alive, where sin is seen as sin and where it is removed and obliterated by the mighty Spirit who rules the Church. And we believe in life everlasting, in the enduring life that is revealed in this love of Christ Jesus, in this Church of the Holy Spirit, in this forgiveness of sin.

Worship meeting, Rhön Bruderhof, Aug. 5, 1935

Jesus gave us two symbolic actions of special significance. One is the communal eating and drinking (the Lord's Supper); the other is washing by pouring over or by immersion (baptism). One is nourishment, the other cleansing. The act of cleansing or purifying is linked with the sign of death, of laying in the earth and raising up again. This symbol of baptism, therefore, contains two pictures: the pouring over of water, meaning cleansing and purification; and immersion in water, meaning death, burial, and resurrection.

Rhön Bruderhof, Jan. 8, 1933

JESUS GIVES NEW LIFE

Christ is the new life. He meets us at every turn of our lives. If we submit to Christ's influence, He shows us that everything good we ever intended to do or ever did is black and evil, wicked and unjust, in contrast to the only true purity, the only true love and righteousness, that is, Christ Himself. He leads us to repentance, to the point at which all our thinking is turned upside down and we can no longer pretend that black is white or filthy is clean. But Jesus is greater than John the Baptist. His Cross opens up to us the very core of God's heart. In His death God's all-embracing love is disclosed to us, bringing forgiveness and unclouded reconciliation. By uniting with the

Crucified One, we constantly renew our break with all that has been, all that we ever were or have done. Christ shows us our unworthiness, the shameful lovelessness in which our lives have been entangled until this very moment. He removes the fog and the clouds so that in a flash we see the abyss that gapes between our corrupt nature and God's heart. But at the same instant He Himself closes that chasm by the boundless strength of His outstretched arms and pierced hands. By His forgiveness He unites our heart with God's heart.

"Neues Leben," Das neue Werk, *1920/21*

REBIRTH AND THE KINGDOM OF THE FUTURE

We all love the third chapter of John's Gospel, but we tend to forget that the context of this personal rebirth is God's Kingdom—it goes beyond the individual. The coming of God's Kingdom is the all-important thread that runs through the Bible, and we need to be filled and overwhelmed by this promise for the future. (Isa. 11:1–10) The Holy Spirit wants to overpower us and fill us and lead us into the coming Kingdom. He brings to life Jesus' words about the future and helps us to become a living example, a picture, or a visible witness of the coming Kingdom.

Letter, Mar. 1935

We belong to the King of the heavenly Kingdom, and so our life should be like His. The question to each one is: Will you go the way of the Cross, or not? Are you willing to be baptized with the baptism with which I was baptized, to drink the cup that I have drunk? (Mark 10:38–39)

Meeting with guests, Rhön Bruderhof, Aug. 9, 1934

A BREAK WITH THE STATUS QUO

The Risen One gave His disciples instructions to go forth into all the world and proclaim the Gospel of all creation, to call for repentance, to baptize people as a sign that they have broken with all the powers of this world and have entered the fellowship of death and resurrection in the new Kingdom. (Matt. 28:19–20)

Rhön Bruderhof, 1933

Baptism means breaking with the status quo, the power system.

It means dying to the evil life that is part of the violent spirit around us.

It means giving up a life that uses violent means to assert itself.

It means denying the natural urge within us to use power and violence.

It means saying good-bye forever to the desire for worldly wealth and possessions; that includes the sexual desire to possess.

It means putting an end to a sensual, impure way of life that destroys the true life given by God.

Worship meeting, Alm Bruderhof, June 2, 1935

The break is so radical that there can be no question of compromise. (James 4:4) The old, established ways must be completely abandoned and something quite different, quite revolutionary, has to be brought into the midst of it all. (Eph. 4:22–24) That is the task we take up in baptism, the task of mission, of spreading the promise that the Ruler of all worlds to come will assert His authority here and now, wherever this baptism is practiced and this mission is fulfilled.

Rhön Bruderhof, Jan. 8, 1933

DO LITTLE CHILDREN NEED BAPTISM?

Little children are not damned. We are certain that they are united with God because Christ's love excludes no one, and He gave His life for them too. God loves all children, all who have the childlike Spirit on earth as in heaven. (Matt. 19:13–15) God wants us all to be children, filled with the childlike Spirit of Jesus Christ.

Children do not need baptism, for baptism is a sign of repentance, forgiveness, and renewal. It is a sign that the Holy Spirit is given to one who did not have the Spirit because his or her former life was evil.

At baptism we recognize and clearly testify to our innermost conviction of sin, and we experience that God is merciful, that our sins are forgiven, that we repent of our evil, that we believe in the coming Kingdom, and that all worlds will one day be transformed.

Little children should not be burdened with all this. They have not yet entered the sphere where Satan and his spirit of hostility are embattled against God and His Spirit of peace. They are still sheltered in Christ's childlike Spirit.

Worship meeting, Rhön Bruderhof, Jan. 20, 1935

But, it will be objected, the child lives in original sin, though personally innocent. That is true. But original sin in little children means, first, that they have an inherited tendency to evil as well as to good; and second, that they are subject to physical death, like all human beings. For illness and death came into the world through sin, which is separation from God, the Living One. And to our sorrow all our children have inherited it; they are mortal. If we were in perfect fellowship with God, the Ever Living; if we were motivated by the living Spirit to do good and only good in free and lively activity; if we had remained in God's life, in His love, without any clouding of the living relationship to God's power—then we would not be mortal.

Worship meeting, Rhön Bruderhof, June 28, 1935

Infants are not capable of confessing their faith or of choosing the way of Christ by a conscious decision. So we cannot really speak of a baptismal covenant for these little ones. They can have no understanding of creation. How much less are they able to grasp that this creation is fallen! How much less are they able to grasp that Christ really came and that He brought full freeing and healing!

How much less are they able to grasp the Holy Spirit, who comes over the Church and creates complete unanimity!

Quite apart from this, infants have no need of baptism because (as we have seen) the covenant of baptism is based on repentance. It means turning away from the evil, corrupt ways of our time, breaking with the sin and injustice of this world. Infants know nothing of all that, so how can they make this break or find repentance?

This leads us to the deepest mystery we feel with regard to infants. Christ Jesus died for our sins, for the sins of the whole world, and His sacrifice brings a reconciliation and uniting that embraces the whole world. (John 1:29) We need daily the forgiveness of sins, which Jesus Christ brought about through His death, reconciling us completely with God. Now little babies have never yet done anything intentionally. Everything they do is instinctive. So the reconciliation Jesus brought about for the whole world is valid for all infants and little children. This very important truth is denied by the inclusive Churches. They maintain that unbaptized infants are damned by the curse of original sin. We do not believe this, for Jesus Christ took little children in His arms, caressed and kissed them, and said, "Unless you become like these little children, you cannot enter the Kingdom of Heaven. The Kingdom of God belongs to the little children." (Matt. 18:3; Mark 10:14–16) . . . .

We have no doubt that little children by their very nature belong to the Kingdom of God—just because they are little children. And in case they should die at an early age, they will be members of the Kingdom of God straightaway, for the reconciliation is theirs too; they are accepted into God's Kingdom.

Worship meeting, Rhön Bruderhof, Jan. 11, 1934

The Lord's Supper

DO THIS IN REMEMBRANCE OF ME

The Lord's Supper is our way of expressing the central experience in Jesus, because we do not want to forget Jesus. How easy it is for us to forget Him! We need a very powerful reminder of Him. That is why we need the Lord's Supper; it is a Meal of Remembrance. (1 Cor. 11:23–25)

What does the Meal of Remembrance point to? That Jesus is not forgotten, that His death is proclaimed. In the Lord's Supper the united Body of the Church is set apart from any other body, any other organism, any outward association of people. In the Lord's Supper we acknowledge that this Body of the Church is alive, that it is of God, and that it belongs to Jesus.

Worship meeting, Alm Bruderhof, June 2, 1935

The Teaching of the Twelve Apostles was written down during the second century in an attempt to retain the earliest memories from the time of the apostles. It gives the following picture as part of a thanksgiving prayer at the Lord's Supper: The seeds of grain are scattered over many fields, and then comes harvest time. The grain from one field does not necessarily come together in one loaf. Mostly it is grain from many fields in different places that is baked together into one loaf. So we are many people; we have come together from many nations, from many different strata in society, from a variety of ideologies and traditions. (Rev. 5:9–10) We come from many different fields, but we are baked together in one loaf. . . .

Before the bread can be baked, the grain brought together from the various fields in different areas has to be ground. Unless the grain is ground, there will be no loaf; each grain must be ground. If one remains unground, it will be a whole grain in the loaf, and when the loaf is served, someone will take a knife and remove that grain because it is out of place in the bread. It has kept its own nature, its individual existence, its own importance.

When the grain is ground, the flour is put in a hot oven to bake, and only then does it become bread. Then it is placed on the table. And if it is a truly communal table, the bread is for all to share. Then we cannot pray, "Give me today my daily bread." Rather, we pray together, "Give us the bread we need each day." For us all, every day! (Matt. 6:11)

Then the bread is broken and shared. Once again community is stressed, this time in the sharing of the bread. The risen Jesus was recognized by the way He broke bread and distributed it at the common table. (Luke 24:30–31)

The same things are said of the wine. The grapes must be crushed in the winepress because the wine would be spoiled if one grape were to hold on to its own existence. One wine has to be made out of them all. So each grape has to give itself up in the ultimate sacrifice for the unity of the wine. Just as the whole community shares one loaf, so too it shares one cup. . . .

The Lord's Supper is a reminder of the perfect sacrifice made by this one grain that is ground, this one grape that is crushed—the One that makes all the difference. It is the proclamation of His death until He returns, the expectation of that final future when He will again eat the bread and drink the wine with us in His Kingdom. (Matt. 26:29)

Alm Bruderhof, May 1934
(See The Early Christians, *pp. 181–189)*

SYMBOLISM IN THE LORD'S SUPPER

The common hearth and communal eating and drinking are characteristic of humankind; communal work and communal households around the fire developed as a result.

In the last supper Jesus held, these ordinary, simple things were given a depth of meaning that points to ultimate truth. Bread and wine were combined in this meal, the one basic and nourishing, the other noble and fiery. Bread and wine, not bread and water, as ascetics would prefer. Jesus was not an ascetic, not even in regard to strong drink. In our eating and drinking too, He wants us to combine simplicity with real joy in God's gifts to us. According to the age-old custom of simple folk, the loaf is passed around, and each person breaks off a piece and passes it on to the next. The wine jug is passed around, and each person drinks from it and passes it on. There can hardly be a more powerful expression of community than this time-honored custom of passing the single loaf and the single jug of wine from one to the other.

Let us look at these symbols. The singleness of the loaf and of the wine, and the red color of the wine, calling to mind the life-blood of a human body, are powerful symbols of the communal meal. The loaf is broken; the wine flows in streams. Unity is a visible reality, uniting is complete: "This is my body, and this is my blood." (1 Cor. 11:24–26)

To be sure, that is a message so simple and so radical that the proud intellect cannot tolerate it. This message shows God's will, which is for us to be united, to be broken for the sake of unity. Just as Jesus let His body be broken and His blood be shed, He wants you to give up being a separate grain of wheat, a separate grape. He wants you to throw yourself into the unity of the Body, the unity of the flowing wine; He wants you to go through the death of Christ. Unity will then be created, the new Spirit will flow and give life to the Body, making it of one heart and one mind. This is the mystery of Christ, of the Church, the mystery of complete unity. This is the Lord's Supper.

Rhön Bruderhof, Jan. 8, 1933

When Jesus instituted the Meal of Remembrance, He spoke of surrendering His life and sacrificing His blood and His body. There is a deep connection between the events of that last supper—eating the sacrificial lamb, eating the bread, and drinking the wine—and Jesus' proclamation of forgiveness, unity, and the future Kingdom. These all belong together.

Jesus used the sacrifice of the lamb to explain to those gathered with Him at table what the sacrifice for God's Kingdom is. In doing so He proclaimed His own sacrificial death. (1 Cor. 5:7; Acts 8:32–33) So for us as for the first Christians, everything we eat becomes a thanksgiving for a sacrifice. Every meal together is a communal lovemeal, a thank-offering, a meal of remembrance. We should give great thanks to God each time we gather for a meal. What we give thanks for is not that our own appetites, our own interests, are satisfied. We give thanks for the sacrifice of the plants and animals God gives us so that we may live for unity, which is God's will; so that our lives are sustained and we can go on witnessing to God's Kingdom by living in the communal Church.

Meeting with guests, Alm Bruderhof, Sept. 16, 1934

Worship

Silent prayer is a deep necessity for every Church community, especially in times when something sweeps over us, when God's wind blows over us, for it is important that we recognize what God wants to say. We need to hear His voice in the events around us and in our midst. We need to hear His voice in our hearts. And in times like ours, in the midst of the darkness that has descended on the earth, we need to see His light.

Rhön Bruderhof, July 1933

Silent inner gathering for worship is an essential part of our common life. That does not mean that we have to spend a certain length of time together during which we may neither speak nor sing. On the contrary, we believe that words of faith and love and deeds of faith and love are born out of the common silence. When we are silent, we want to be silent before God. What we should silence are our own words, our own deeds. All that has arisen or may arise from our self-will should be laid down during silent worship.

Meeting with guests, Alm Bruderhof, Mar. 3, 1935

Our common silence is deeply akin to a Quaker meeting. In our meetings we long that God Himself speak to us, that Christ's voice speak among us, that the Holy Spirit move our hearts directly. That is why the quiet and silence are so very important to us. Human talk often drives away the Spirit. But in the common silence God fills us directly. We testify to this as the deepest experience of our life together. When we listen to the voice of God within us, we find unqualified unanimity. When we listen deep down to what the Spirit says to the Church, the same truth and love will grip us all. Then the right words will be given; what God says to us in the silence will be voiced, out of the depths of the Spirit.

Worship meeting, Rhön Bruderhof, Aug. 3, 1935

We should be ready to put our trust in God. Then out of the gathered silence words may come from us, words that come out of the depths of our hearts, out of ultimate truth and truthfulness. When people can be silent together, words of ultimate truth can come out of this silence. When people can be silent before God and He speaks to them, they may be able to say words that are given to them, that do not come from themselves.

Alm Bruderhof, Mar. 4, 1935

It is startling to realize that the very prayer Jesus entrusted to His disciples has been turned into its opposite by the literalistic spirit. Jesus summed up just in these few words what God's will is, to warn His disciples not to use many words nor to imagine that an unnatural display is a part of prayer.

Worship meeting, Rhön Bruderhof, Jan. 27, 1935

The misuse of meaningful songs, or even only a lack of understanding and feeling in singing them communally, has a devastating effect. When we sing them in real community with the Holy Spirit, we sense something of innermost holiness. Such songs should be sung only at very special moments, only at times of God-given experiences. To suggest songs that were once written in the Spirit, with the idea of producing an atmosphere that does not exist, to sing "God is present with us!" when no one feels that God really is present, to dare to sing "Lord of all, to Thee we bow" when there is no real honoring of God's greatness in the atmosphere of the meeting is a misuse that borders on the sin against the Holy Spirit.

Members' meeting, Rhön Bruderhof, Aug. 21, 1935

Jesus said, "The hour is coming, and is already here, when people will worship the Father in spirit and in truth." (John 4:23) He contrasts "spirit and truth" with church buildings, bell towers, domes, and synagogues, as much as to say, till now people have prayed in temples, on mountain tops, or in sacred groves; now they will worship God in spirit and in truth. Strange contrast!

Why should we not make use of solemnly consecrated places or rooms to worship God in spirit and in truth? For the very reason that such places have been connected for thousands of years with the misuse of God's name. They house a subtle form of idolatry that clings legalistically to a certain book or to some image or idolatrous rite. The cult of consecrated places is a threat to the worship in spirit and in truth. The more incense, the more imagery, the more tradition and prescribed words, the less spirit and truth.

Worship meeting, Rhön Bruderhof, Jan. 27, 1935

We fully affirm prayer and worship; only we are cautious about them in a wider circle, out of reverence for prayer. We have our worship meetings in a united circle.

Meeting with guests, Rhön Bruderhof, Aug. 22, 1935

If you have had a quarrel with a brother or a sister that leaves a tension between you, then these words of Jesus apply: "If, when you are bringing your gift to the altar, you suddenly remember that your brother had a grievance against you, leave your gift where it is before the altar. First go and make your peace with your brother, and only then come back and offer your gift." (Matt. 5:23–24, NEB) Unimpaired unity is essential to the Spirit of the Church. And the prayer of the Church presupposes that those who are met together are wholly united with one another and with the Spirit of the Church. Should there be a tension between any members, it is the obligation of each one to resolve it straightaway, at the very latest during the time the community is gathering.

Rhön Bruderhof, 1932

The important thing is that we are united about the object of our prayer. Jesus says, "If two or three of you agree in asking for anything, it will be granted to you by my Father in heaven." (Matt. 18:19–20) If two or three ask God for something to happen, it will happen. It is not the words we use that matter, but our unity. There is no need for many words giving an exact description; God needs no explanation from us. What matters is that the members of a Church reach complete agreement about the object of their prayer before they join in calling upon Him.

Worship meeting, Rhön Bruderhof, Jan. 27, 1935

We need to ask the Holy Spirit for His gifts. But we should ask for what the Holy Spirit Himself wants to do in the Church—not, for instance, that any one member wishes to have this or that spiritual gift for himself or herself personally. Rather, each one should ask the Spirit to pour out the horn of plenty over His Church and to give what has been intended for each one since the beginning of time. (1 Cor. 12:27ff)

Let us lay down all self-will and be ready to receive and use whatever gift is given us. Let us be thankful to be allowed to live in simple discipleship of Jesus without being led into temptation by great gifts. And finally let us ask that we all without distinction be given the gift promised to all members of the Body of Christ—the highest of gifts, which is love; that is to say, we ask for the gift of the Holy Spirit. (1 Cor. 13:13)

Worship meeting, June 20, 1934

Mission

NOW IS THE HOUR

The colossal need facing humankind in this hour of history makes it urgent to show a new way. The time is here for the communal Church to be a light on the lampstand, a city on a hill. (Matt. 5:14–15) The reality of the God-given life among us must affect many and finally all people. The time is here when the message of God's unity, justice, and brotherhood in His Kingdom must be spread abroad. But we are exceedingly weak, and our numbers are small, very small, when we think of the magnitude of this calling. . . .

We cannot evade the call of Jesus or the impulse of our hearts. It is a call that goes out to all, especially to all the needy. And when the misery reaches such a pitch as we see around us today, the call of Jesus becomes all the more insistent and pressing—more so than ever before: "Go ye out into all the world!" (Mark 16:15) Go out, get to work! Call the people and gather them in! Now is the hour!

Rhön Bruderhof, Summer 1932

A MISSION TO ALL MEN

The great tidings entrusted to the Church of Christ must be brought to everyone without exception. Everyone should hear it. That does not mean that everybody is expected to join the communal Church of Christ at this particular moment in history. It does mean, though, that the message of truth shall reach every single human being—namely, that this unity in Christ, as it is shown in the life of the communal Church, is the goal of humankind's history. (John 17:20–23) And this message will leave its mark in the depths of every heart, whether or not a person is ready today for the Church of Christ.

Rhön Bruderhof, May 31, 1934

Each one in the Church must live by his vision of the coming Kingdom. Those sent away on sales trips or on training do not have the task of zealously buttonholing people to bring about a personal change in their lives. They are expected to have a vision beyond themselves, looking to the greatness of God's coming Kingdom, but not pressing others. We are heralds of the final Kingdom; from where we are, we go out as bearers of the cause, as envoys of God's Kingdom. The turning of all things is near. Everything else must collapse. God's love alone shall triumph! In doing this task we need at all times to be so turned toward the world around us that we are able to say a word from God; a word coined and weighed to fit the present historical hour. It has to be a word for all nations, proclaiming the suprapolitical Kingdom of God.

Letter, July 1934; English translation:
Sendbrief from the Alm Bruderhof, *pp. 41–42*

We believe that every human being has a longing for true justice, true love and unity. Therefore, the open door of the community is open to everyone. At the same time we realize that not every person is ready for community at every stage of his or her life. You can't expect everyone to be able to accept it at every moment. For example, I can't simply stand at the Leipzigerstrasse in Berlin and call, "Come here, all of you, come and live at the Bruderhof!" It is not cowardice that keeps us from doing this. It would be folly; many people would simply not be in the position to understand such a call. They would not be mature enough in their inner development to follow it. God must call them first. I have no right to call people unless the Spirit Himself has already called them.

Rhön Bruderhof, Oct. 8, 1933

Perhaps the kind of mission we should ask for is a mission to the homeless, to those who live in terrible conditions, close to starvation. That would be preaching the Gospel to the poor in a special way. I believe it is our duty to give every Samaritan service asked of us. But I also believe we need special guidance to seek out the destitute, knowing that they may not be called as yet. It needs to be a mission of mercy and compassion. (Isa. 61:1)

Alm Bruderhof, July 1935

If we are no longer here for all people, if we can no longer concern ourselves with the need and suffering of the whole world, community life has lost its right to exist.

Rhön Bruderhof, May 12, 1935

The powers of bloodshed and violence, of impurity and unfaithfulness, of lying and mammon, have gained more strength than at any other time. And now the truth of Jesus' words becomes clear: The last day will not come until the Gospel of all creation has been proclaimed in all the world. (Matt. 24:14) This Gospel proclaims a new creation, a new day of creation.

It is more than high time that this Gospel be proclaimed to all people and all nations. The Church is charged with carrying out this task. The apostles were sent out by the Church. How can they go unless they are sent? How can they be sent without an authority to send them? How can they proclaim peace unless they have gone forth from a place of peace and bring peace with them? (Rom. 10:15)

Worship meeting, Rhön Bruderhof, Feb. 21, 1935

WHEN SALT LOSES ITS SAVOR

People often raise the following objection to the community life of the Bruderhof. They say we are supposed to be the salt of the earth, and that salt shouldn't be sprinkled in big lumps but in tiny grains. And so the salt of individual Christians should be scattered abroad.

That sounds very convincing. But there are two things wrong with it. First, it is a mistake to think that the community does not act as salt outside its own circle; in fact, people are constantly being sent out. Second, one could ask whether many don't lose their salt-power because of the compromises they cannot avoid making, because of the dangerous mixture of spirits that surrounds them. The sharpness of the salt-power loses its edge. (Matt. 5:13) Things get blurred. People get used to coming to terms with the various trends they encounter, and gradually the clarity of their witness is lost.

Meeting with guests, Rhön Bruderhof, Dec. 30, 1934

And so we understand why life in community is of such tremendous importance and why it is a mistake when people tell us, "You could be much more effective if each one of you lived in a different town; that would give you many more points of contact." The secret of community life does not lie in adding up the number of people who come together. Nor are these people capable by themselves of doing what community life enables them to do. The secret of life in community is the uniting with the invisible cloud of the Spirit, given to people who can wait, wait for God—their all in all.

Rhön Bruderhof, May 12, 1935

THE WAY OF MISSION

When the apostles went out into the world, they did not use persuasion or try to overpower people's minds or wills. The apostles came innocent and harmless as doves. (Matt. 10:16) That was the way they did their mission work. They were sent out like the simplest of creatures, the most unassuming sacrificial birds, like lambs or doves.

And yet they were to be wise as the wisest of animals, provided their cleverness and presence of mind did not conflict with guilelessness and goodness. So they had to be fully aware of what they were getting into. Jesus said, "Do not judge." (Matt. 7:1) Do not set yourselves up to pronounce a final judgment over people. But He also said to judge everything according to the spirit and take a clear stand. "Test the spirits, whether they are from God." (1 John 4:1) You will recognize everything by its fruits. Be discerning, and especially discern the false prophets who come in sheep's clothing. They are ravening wolves, who will soon reveal their true nature. Beware of everything that bears a human face, for the traitor

will appear out of the ranks of those whom you may innocent-
ly trust most, from among your best friends. You will be be-
trayed, arrested, and handed over to the powers that be by
those from whom you least expect it.

Rhön Bruderhof, Jan. 1935

Our fight is not against flesh and blood but against an atmosphere. (Eph. 6:12) This is all-important: the atmosphere
that comes from us has to be stronger and purer and therefore
more victorious than the impure atmosphere usually found
among people. That is why nobody should go out independent
of the Church. No one should dare to go on a mission journey
unless equipped for it by the Holy Spirit. (Mark 13:11; Acts
13:2–4)

Members' meeting, Rhön Bruderhof, Nov. 13, 1934

Jesus formed the core of innermost community with the
twelve, and together they went out to people in the country-
side around. On this we pattern our community life and our
mission.

One of our youngest members, who has felt the call to go
out to people in the neighboring towns, writes about the amazing encounters he is having. During most of the year three or
four brothers are away on such journeys. It is a small attempt
to reach out to people, but it needs a direct inspiration in the
hearts of those who are to be sent out, and it can only be done
with the full agreement of the whole Church community.

Meeting with guests, Rhön Bruderhof, Aug. 14, 1935

We are all united in our deepest concern that Christ himself may send you out. (Matt. 9:38) May He lead you step by

step to one task after another. We ask that you may be protect-
ed so that your heart and your tongue do not run away with
you in an exuberance of feeling or eloquent words. Rather,
you will need to be inspired to speak the right word at the
right time, when the person you meet has reached the point
when he or she is full of expectation, when he or she is at last
ready to hear and accept just this word. It is our earnest prayer
that you may be led in this way. Our thoughts will go with you
and support you day and night. . . .

There are dangers on the way of mission, for instance the
danger of idealizing community life. My wish for you is that
you represent only what is reality in your life and in our common life. (1 John 1:3)

Members' meeting, Rhön Bruderhof, Nov. 13, 1934

The Church can be compared to a lantern with a light
burning and shining in it. The light shines out through the lantern glass to all the world. The rays of light are brothers and
sisters sent out on mission. They are messengers of God, messengers of light, angels of light, apostles of light, light-rays of
the Gospel sent out by the light of the Church, the lovelight of
God in Christ Jesus, in His Holy Spirit. This comparison
shows us that the messengers sent out are not independent,
they do not undertake anything on their own. And the Church
community is not shut in on itself and does not undertake anything for its own sake. It is its nature to shine, to send out
light.

Worship meeting, Rhön Bruderhof, Oct. 22, 1935

OUR WORK IS VERY SMALL

How very small our work is in comparison with the tremendous suffering in the world and in the light of the great

events of history. I think it is very important to realize this. All the more we depend on prayer that in this world with all its billions of people, our modest efforts to sell our books and turnery will have some impact on the world in ways known only to God. (Luke 10:2)

Members' meeting, Rhön Bruderhof, June 24, 1934

Mission has to be a challenge addressed only to people who are in some measure already drawn by God. No one can come to Him unless the Father draws him. (John 6:44) God is the great awakener. Through the events of history He strikes with hammer blows. But it is not for us to shatter consciences. Our task is to seek, find, and gather those people and groups who are inwardly moved.

Members' meeting, Rhön Bruderhof, July 18, 1931

The call goes out to everyone. Whoever seriously wants to be a Christian will find a warm welcome here, anyone who wants to devote his or her short life to love, who wants to give up a basically futile existence and leave behind all compromise with the world, who wants to follow Jesus and nobody but Jesus.

Alm Bruderhof leaflet, May 1934

There is a hidden Christ in some who claim they are unbelievers. We have experienced that Christ is strongly at work in people who still deny Him with their lips. That shows how much greater Christ is than our minds can imagine, how much more loving He is than our hearts can grasp. (1 John 3:20) But that should not surprise us. If we have experienced even a little of Christ's Spirit, we will not ask all those we meet whether they believe as we do. Our love for them will urge us to visit them and to find out what is alive in their hearts and to acknowledge this before there is ever any talk of unity.

Alm Bruderhof, May 27, 1935

IN THE FOOTSTEPS OF JESUS

Simple, apostolic mission does not require large halls and grand lectures. It is much simpler than that. It means finding the living thread from one person to another, from house to house, from one town to the next. It means discovering the footsteps of Jesus Christ to see which way He went, so that we can go to the very place where He has been. And to find that is sheer grace. . . .

It has to be said that the main thing is not gathering individuals or little groups to live in full community. That would not accord with the greatness of God. The main purpose of mission is to make all the world aware of who God is and what His will is, of His power to bring about perfect love through Jesus Christ, and that this love can be put into practice here and now in a community life. And that, today, unity can be lived out in complete social justice and brotherliness. The main thing is that the whole world, and that includes those in high places as well as the masses of underprivileged, know that something that had almost been forgotten is after all a reality and still possible.

Worship meeting, Rhön Bruderhof, Nov. 21, 1934

THE INDIVIDUAL
AND THE COMMUNITY

Whitsun conference, Sannerz, 1921

The Body of Believers

Life in God means gathering. (John 12:32) God's life wants to gather us into an organism; He unites us in one living body, animated by the Holy Spirit. (1 Cor. 12:13–14) So our unity in the Spirit and our bond of peace are the driving force in our daily, practical life, and that is where our unity becomes physical reality.

Meeting with guests, Rhön Bruderhof, Aug. 12, 1935

We believe that the Holy Spirit reveals His presence in the living Church community. This is where our Christianity differs from a purely personal one. True, the individual heart must be visited by the Holy Spirit. Yet the Spirit's actual working begins in the communal Church. When the experience of the individual heart is shared by the whole believing community, then, and only then, will the Kingdom of God be visible.

Meeting with guests, Alm Bruderhof, July 25, 1935

If anyone asks us whether we, a few weak and needy people living in community, are the Church, we have to say no, we are not. Like all human beings, we are the recipients of God's love. And like everybody else—more so, if anything—we are unworthy and unfit for the working of the Holy Spirit, for the building of the Church, and for the mission to all the world.

But if anyone puts the question this way, "Does the Church come to you? Does the Church of God come down where you are, to people? Is the Church present in the Holy Spirit, who alone has the power to bring the Church down?" then we have to answer yes, that is so. The Church comes down wherever believers are gathered who have no other will, no other purpose, but that God's Kingdom come and that the Church of Jesus Christ be revealed in the unity of His Spirit. The Church is wherever the Holy Spirit is. (1 John 3:24)

Rhön Bruderhof, Mar. 1, 1933

The Church is a living structure, made up of live building stones. They are far from perfect; they need to be dressed and hewn if they are to fit into the building. And yet it is a perfect building. The mystery is this: the life of this building does not reside in its parts, but rather in the living, gathering Holy Spirit. Its unity does not result from assembling the parts that make it up or from an agreement of opinions. By nature the stones are spiritually dead. But the Holy Spirit awakens them to life by joining them together in a new unity. (1 Pet. 2:5)

Rhön Bruderhof, July 30, 1933

If only we could challenge the heads of government in our day as George Fox challenged Oliver Cromwell to refuse the crown and lay it down before the throne of Jesus Christ!*

---

*In his *Journal*, George Fox refers to his meeting with Oliver Cromwell, who had been offered the crown of England. "I said again, they that sought to put on him a crown would take away his life; and I bid him mind the crown that was immortal." See *The Journal of George Fox*, with introduction by Rufus M. Jones (London: J.M. Dent and Sons Ltd., 1962), p. 170.

But first we have to lay down all our own little wreaths at Christ's throne, including our glittering self-will and all our personal wishes and presumptions. And the dwelling place of the communal Church, the place of unity, is where this is made easy for us. It is impossible for our selfish nature to triumph when we are confronted with the Church. Selfish desire cannot possibly impose itself where there is unanimity. In the unity of the Church we will be freed from all the delusions to which we are so prone. In the Church of Jesus Christ all pomposity falls silent and all personal self-importance is blotted out. (Eph. 4:17–24)

Worship meeting, Rhön Bruderhof, Sept. 4, 1933

That a person changes in the course of his life is certainly human; but it is more than that: it is in accordance with God's will. Since we will never measure up to God's perfection on any level, we must constantly change. It is the direction of our change that is decisive. We are told what this direction should be: to move closer to the image of God and in Christ to grow deeper in our understanding of it so that He can work within us and change us. (2 Cor. 3:18) But the image of God cannot be mirrored by one single individual; it is mirrored by an organic unity composed of many members who are committed to one another and support one another. That organic unity is the Church animated by the Holy Spirit. The Body of Christ is the image of God in our time.

Mealtime at the Rhön Bruderhof, Jan. 30, 1933

We in all our smallness are allowed to live on this earth in the Church; there we can reflect the Father's nature in word, life, and work. Not the individual believer, but the Church, whose orderly plan is given by God through His instruments, is the new Body of Christ. It is the new embodiment and form of the Word made man. Here, prayer to God—the ruling, commanding, helping, and loving "Thou"—subjects the rebellious resistance of the human "I" within the "we" of the Church, with complete trust and faith, to the almighty, all-uniting God. He will always remain the utterly different, the only great and good One. Through His Spirit He speaks and calls again and again to the Church. He gives it His grace and protection and equips and commissions it.

1929; English translation: Prayer Life, *pp. 13–14*

Jesus wanted to have His closest friends, those we call His disciples, constantly near Him. (Mark 3:13–14) Later on, His Spirit impelled the first Christians to stay close together so that they might live the life Jesus lived and do the deeds He did. (Acts 2:42–47) Since they were driven by a deep inner compulsion, every question or problem in their life together had to find a solution whose outer form was perfectly in keeping with complete unity and love.

Bible study session, 1919

The all-powerful presence of Christ in His Church was the secret of the early Christian communities. (Col. 1:26–27) The wonderful thing about this mystery was that Christ did not appear as a vision but was Himself present because the Holy Spirit was poured out over them.

At the very moment when members of the Church acknowledge that God's love is poured into their hearts through the Holy Spirit, they are acknowledging that Christ is present, He is there! He triumphs over all impure spirits and emotional ties, over touchiness and selfishness, over all sin. The King, the Crucified and Risen One, is present in His Church through His powerful Spirit.

Members' meeting, Rhön Bruderhof, Nov. 2, 1935

The bond with the Brotherhood is not a human bond based on a mutual promise. Rather, it is the necessary outward sign that we yield in faith to God's will and to the Holy Spirit. God's will is that we be fully one, and it is the Holy Spirit who makes this unity among us an actual fact over and over again.

Rhön Bruderhof, Jan. 13, 1933

We are not a collection of people who have good intentions about living in community and think that if all these good intentions are led in the right direction, the result will be something like unity in the Spirit. That is not what we believe. We know that in spite of our incapacity for communal living, in spite of our weaknesses of character and our lack of gifts, in spite of the way we are, the Spirit of Jesus Christ, who is the Spirit of unity, calls us to this way and bids us gather others.

Meeting with guests, Rhön Bruderhof, Nov. 3, 1932

There is no particular individual who gives orders to others; that would amount to a division between employer and employee. We don't have that. And we don't have a group of intellectuals ruling over people who do the physical work. That would divide us into groups, one superior to the other. Every remnant of division into class, caste, or rank is thoroughly rooted out. Such organization of our work as is needed is born of unanimity in the Church community. The only superior authority is this unanimity, this full accord of all believing and loving members. . . .

Some members have a specific service assigned to them, such as the Servant of the Word, steward, business manager, work distributor, housemother, school principal, and many others. But these can carry out their service only to the extent that it is supported by the full agreement of the community. The organizing that results from this causes no problems for anyone in the community. On joining the community each one brings into the unity everything he is and has. He keeps nothing, not a single hour of working time, no savings account, however small, not even the tiniest box of valuables. He owns absolutely nothing. (Luke 12:32–34) What he has in his possession is only given to him to use as long as he needs it to do his work. But this does not make for uniformity; we should not imagine that communal organization results in just one single note; it leads to rich harmony.

The community provides the means for each member to produce fruitful work in farm and garden, craft and art work, publishing and printing, teaching and recreation, kindergarten and nursery groups, kitchen and laundry, housecleaning, and so forth. Everyone does his job for the entire community.

Meeting with guests, Rhön Bruderhof, Oct. 6, 1932

It is a real miracle that we have been able to live these twelve years in community, that we have known the power of the freeing, redeeming, healing Spirit and are able to testify to that power. A miracle like this can never come from us.

How can we enter into the atmosphere of this miracle? We find the answer in the words of a favorite song of the Sannerz time: "In holy waiting we're at home." We are at home in active dedication, and we know with certainty that the Holy Spirit, the perfect nature of Jesus, will come to us. What happened when the Holy Spirit came? The fact that we have to wait a long time need not discourage anyone. The little band in Jerusalem had to go through a very difficult time of waiting that must have seemed almost endless, and then it happened: The Holy Spirit was poured out. (Acts 1:4–5; 2:1–4) All at once everything changed. And we believe that this change has to take place again and again.

Rhön Bruderhof, Aug. 30, 1931

Today we have again reminded ourselves that we by no means see our Brotherhood as the goal, but as our stake toward the goal. We have no thought of consolidating the Brotherhood for the sake of the Brotherhood, or the Bruderhof for the sake of the Bruderhof. We want our Brotherhood to go into action for peace and unity so that the whole world with all its nations may attain to the Kingdom of justice and peace. In other words, we want to work for the Kingdom of justice and peace to come over the whole world. Then the monstrous powers of animosity and bitterness will be opposed by a little band, however small, that sends rays of unity, peace, justice, brotherliness, and humaneness out into the world, rays of God's love and Christ's love, rays of Kingdom power. That is what we want to live for, and that is the object of your uniting with us.

Meeting with guests, Rhön Bruderhof, Sept. 15, 1935

Leadership and Service

WHAT IS A SERVANT?

There is no lord or master in the Church except Christ, there is no leader but Jesus Christ, who is the Head. We are all brothers one with another. We are all members, each one serving the others. (Matt. 23:8–12) We are living cells. Governing this Body with the power of the Holy Spirit is Jesus Christ, Son of the Living God.

Rhön Bruderhof, July 30, 1933

In New Testament times, the days of Greco-Roman and Oriental slave culture, servants were not only those who served at table and acted as personal servants, kitchen boys, and house servants. Even scholars, poets, language teachers, accountants, business managers, and head stewards freely served their masters as slaves. That is what the apostles had in mind when they spoke of the Servants of the Church.* (Gal. 5:13) . . .

What does the service mean for all those who are ap-

---

*Authentic leadership in Christian community is service. Therefore the Bruderhof uses the old Hutterian designation, Servant of the Word, instead of minister or pastor. The words servant, deacon, and minister are all translations of the same word *diakonos* in the New Testament.

pointed to be true Servants of the Church? The apostles gave the name of servant or deacon to all those brothers who were charged with important responsibilities in the Church. In our community life, too, servant is the best word to describe any bearer of special responsibility. Servants are those who, while carrying a heavy responsibility for a large part of the communal life, occupy the lowest place in the Church.

The place of the Servant of the Word is truly a burdened one—often overburdened. He does his service in the love of truth and the truth of love. (1 Tim. 6:11) He does it in a brotherly spirit, the spirit in which all brothers and sisters are of equal worth.

Members' meeting, Alm Bruderhof, July 28, 1935

The Shepherd or Elder has the final responsibility for the whole Bruderhof. He is entrusted with the Service of the Word, with concern for the personal welfare of all members, with the main responsibility for the children's education, and with the care of guests. He is accountable for the goods and money and the material welfare of the community. He is expected to follow through all work done by the Bruderhof, both within the community and outside, including mission and printing and publishing. . . .

In both inner and outer matters, the Housemother is given the task of caring for all at the Bruderhof under the guidance of the Elder and in close conjunction with the Steward. As the housekeeper, she is responsible for the running of the house and the women's work.

The Church of God, coming to us in the Spirit and in Christ's future, is called our mother. Therefore there is a unique significance in the loving service to the Church entrusted to our Housemother for all our members and guests.

"Aufbau und Ordnungen," 1929

To have to be Elder or anything similar is a heavy burden; it is an ordeal. Anyone who hankers after it simply does not realize the anguish this service, holy and necessary as it is, brings to us weak human beings. (1 Cor. 9:16) Happy are those who do not have it laid upon them; happy, that is, unless they secretly covet such a service for themselves.

Letter, June 18, 1930

I am willing just simply to live with you all without any claim to be Elder. I don't want any title. If the term Elder is felt to be a title, I shall lay it down. If it is a social position, I hereby renounce this position as a work of the Devil. So I say we must cleanse our consciences of dead works. (Heb. 9:14)

Members' meeting, Rhön Bruderhof, July 6, 1935

AUTHORITY DEPENDS ON THE GIFT OF THE SPIRIT

A Servant of the Spirit has to be commissioned by the Holy Spirit. He must be chosen, called, and sent out by the Holy Spirit and also by a people filled with the Spirit. (Acts 13:2–3) He has to be sent out into God's harvest by God Himself and by His Church. Even Christ was sent and anointed by the Holy Spirit. (Luke 4:18–19) The apostles had to be clothed with power from on high by the living Word before they could go on their travels as Servants of the Word. When the Word is proclaimed, it has to come from the living Bible of the heart. That is what gave the words of the apostles their force, their vigor, the ring of truth. Their words cut to the quick, stabbing like knives.

Talk on Sebastian Frank,
Rhön Bruderhof, Sept. 22, 1933

In the first Church, the men who were appointed as deacons or servants (to make sure everything was distributed fairly) were required to be full of the Holy Spirit and wisdom. (Acts 6:3) Such a man was Stephen. He proved to be a man full of the Holy Spirit to his last moment, when he died as a martyr.

Worship meeting, Rhön Bruderhof, July 13, 1933

We have no fixed offices here, only services that grow out of the stream of love, the moving current of the Spirit. As soon as those who do these services want to be something independent of this stream of love and of the Spirit, their life is a lie, an impossibility. Not even the most gifted person has anything to say if he believes in himself.

Worship meeting, Alm Bruderhof, June 12, 1935

The Holy Spirit wants to give us so much light that we not only obey what He has made clear to us, but that we see further and grasp the movement of heart He inspires at any given moment in other members of the Church, especially in the most childlike.

I could almost say that for one who does the Service of the Word it is more important to perceive at any given moment the voice speaking and the light dawning in other members than to heed his own heart. As soon as he recognizes in any member the movement of heart inspired by this light, he must express it to make it clear to all.

Letter, July 1934; English translation:
Sendbrief from the Alm Bruderhof, pp. 51–52

No Church community has within it the generative power that brings rebirth and new life. Nor is any Servant of the

Word able to give others the chance of new life and the power that comes from it. Were he to believe even the slightest bit that he could, his service would be lost and would have to be laid down. The secret is the Jerusalem above, the mother of us all, who has the power to give new birth. (Gal. 4:26; Rev. 21:2) That is where new life comes from, new justice and righteousness, new love, new vitality.

Worship meeting, Rhön Bruderhof, Jan. 7, 1935

Guests, young people, and novices should feel able to confide in a Servant about their problems whenever necessary. Not that an individual should keep on bringing himself and his feelings to the attention of the Servant of the Word, but whenever emotional problems and spiritual needs keep someone from serving God's Kingdom in full dedication, he should ask a Servant of the Word for help. (Heb. 13:17)

Members' meeting, Rhön Bruderhof, Dec. 4, 1932

The Servant of the Word must never force or press anything on the Church community entrusted to him. He is not placed in the leadership of the Church to do violence to its members, but for their joy. (2 Cor. 1:24)

Rhön Bruderhof, July 26, 1931

DISCERNMENT OF SPIRITS

A ship's pilot has to be at all times in full accord with his whole crew, a gift that is closely analogous to the discernment of spirits. You can't steer clear of rocks unless you realize they are there.

The gift of helmsmanship is a specific spiritual gift needed by every Servant of the Word. Not only do the Servants of
the Word need it; their service has to be supported by many
other people, just as in any ship there are reserves. As many
community members as possible need to be given the gift of
steering the right course in inner as well as in practical matters.

Members' meeting, Rhön Bruderhof, Oct. 20, 1935

Only a Church that is fully awake can survive these dangerous times. (1 Cor. 16:13) We have no moment free for
tiredness, for getting limp and weary and being concerned
with ourselves. Every moment is needed to keep the Church
awake, using the weapons of the Kingdom left and right. Is
that clear? So we must ask God for the spirit of alertness, for
the Holy Spirit. We know we are tired people with weary
flesh. We of ourselves do not have the strength to meet head-
on all the dangers threatening from right and left and to keep
our wits about us in the midst of it all.

And this is where the Servants of the Word need to be
alert and prove their constancy, being watchful in all directions. Then the Church will be kept on the right course by the
freshly blowing wind, the breath of God, the wind of the
Holy Spirit. In these times of danger a gentle breeze is not
enough—a cold, invigorating storm has to come. We must ask
for it to come and drive out all lukewarmness from among us.

Rhön Bruderhof, Dec. 1934

These are the dangers that surround us:

First is bureaucracy and bossdom, the presumption of
brothers who look upon their service as a means to elevate
their own persons. Out of a sense of duty they suppress the

free movement of the Spirit. This threatens to enslave the rest of the community.

Second comes the tendency to arrogant moralism, the audacity of a person who places himself and his moral convictions above others. Consequently he thinks and speaks slightingly of people who are not on the same high moral level.

The third danger is a spirit of business efficiency: the constant concern about earning money, about the harvest, about the productivity of the daily life, about all the hard work that is being done.

And finally there is sheer pride, which is quite logically connected with all the rest: some people think they are the most capable and most discerning and others less competent; other people get depressed when they realize that they cannot reach these high moral levels or such business efficiency.

Worship meeting, Alm Bruderhof, June 12, 1935

ONLY THE SPIRIT SHOULD SPEAK

When we go the holy way of the Church, none of us has the right to do just as he or she chooses, no one has the right to go ahead on his or her own. We have to speak, work, and act by the stimulation of God's Spirit. This is the only way Church community can exist. Therefore, in every Brotherhood meeting and every kind of work as well as in the Service of the Word, the Spirit alone should be able to determine what we say and do.

Once we have fully understood this, we will have deep reverence for the spoken word in our worship meetings or Brotherhood meetings. Then we will not look on people and their human characteristics. Instead we will hear only the voice expressing what God has to say, what God is actually telling us now. And the same applies to deeds. As soon as we deviate by so much as a hair's breadth from the holiness and godliness of the way, even with the best human intentions, we are immediately in extreme danger of drowning in humanness. And linked with this is the danger of the whole city on the hill drowning in the swamp.

Worship meeting, Alm Bruderhof, Sept. 30, 1934

When we are about to read something aloud, we should not do so unless we are really moved by the Holy Spirit. I don't mean that we should use a particularly lofty style of speech, voice, or manner. The prompting of the Holy Spirit may inspire us in quite practical matters, for instance for our workshops or garden layout; or it may help us in personal concerns such as marriage. The prompting of the Holy Spirit can touch on anything and everything that is part of life. But it needs to be born of God's heart and really given to us by God. Otherwise it is better to be silent. (1 Cor. 2:13)

Members' meeting, Rhön Bruderhof, Feb. 23, 1935

Admonition and Forgiveness

ALL MEMBERS OF THE CHURCH NEED HELP

The spirit of joy is a constructive spirit, and the spirit of order and discipline is part of it. Order and discipline in the Church are of the Spirit; they cannot come from human law. It is not a matter of punishment imposed by one person's moral force on another against that person's will. That has become very obvious. Since this kind of correction is out of the question, there need be no fear of punishment. What one ought to feel is not fear but the sincere remorse or innermost pain that comes into the heart after one has failed.

As long as people live in the atmosphere of the Spirit, they will never of their own free will do evil, never deliberately do anything that could disturb the unity and order of what the Spirit has created. (1 John 3:6) But then how does it happen that we can commit blunders or go astray in ways we have not willed or even foreseen? We human beings are weak and stupid. Often we scarcely see the evil approaching. But to stop resisting evil as it comes closer is worse. And it is still more serious if we are resigned to growing disorder or even get used to it by almost imperceptible degrees.

Any member of the Church who gets into this kind of difficulty looks for help, knowing that all members are well aware of the same or similar weaknesses in themselves and are ready at once to help in any way. The entire circle of members wants to help overcome the trouble by nipping it in the bud. Each member believes that the Spirit of Jesus Christ is at work in all members and will not leave anyone in need. (1 Cor. 10:13) Each one who is overcome in a weak point knows that the Church will give support by setting him or her right again.

So it is not right to say that it is enough to recognize the failures in our own hearts and that God will punish us there. This is a mistake because it is only personal. Christ's Church and the Kingdom of God are left out. True, those who are touched by the Spirit realize their faults; those who belong to Jesus and His Church hear God's voice in their hearts, particularly when they have gone wrong. An alert member will feel that the whole Church is affected and shares the responsibility for everything that happens. (1 Cor. 12:25–26) No member of the Church ever feels alone in facing God; each one knows that the whole Church stands with him or her. (Gal. 6:1–2)

Novice meeting, Alm Bruderhof, Sept. 10, 1934

Repentance should lead to changing our hearts, our will, our direction. Exclusion from the Church is not punishment as an end in itself. It is to help us search our hearts deeply and change our lives from the bottom up.

Members' meeting, Rhön Bruderhof, July 1933

JUDGMENT AND FORGIVENESS KEEP THE CHURCH CENTERED

The Holy Spirit convinces the world about judgment. And that brings decision. Judgment consists in the fact that the Prince of this world is judged, not people. (John 16:8–11)

Church discipline never fights against the individual concerned; it fights exclusively against the Prince of this human
world, who is out to enslave souls, including those who belong
to the Church. (2 Tim. 2:24–26)

Worship meeting, Alm Bruderhof, June 28, 1935

You too want good to triumph over evil. But you may be
thinking too much about the persons involved. You see the individual as the main object or as an instrument or a decisive
factor. That is wrong. The battles are between spirits, and persons are affected only insofar as they are the battlefield of
these spiritual powers. To try to help people by sparing them
(that is what we do when we see them in the center) is the
wrong way round. We are missing the main point, which is
that two powers are struggling to win us over: the good,
cleansing Spirit of God and the demonic powers.

Meeting with guests, Rhön Bruderhof, Sept. 15, 1935

Uncompromising discipline is needed to keep the Church
community united and pure. (2 Cor. 11:2) That means a total
rejection of the curse brought by spirits of impurity, possessiveness, lying, murder, and idolatry. The weapons used in this
discipline are brotherly correction and the clear judgment of
the Church.

1928; English translation:
Foundation and Orders 1920–1929, *p. 54*

The Church has authority from God to forgive sins on the
one hand and to exclude on the other. (John 20:23) This is so
that the Church can preserve in true unity what is given it
through the imparting of the Holy Spirit and the coming down

of the Church above. The commission to protect this unity can only be carried out by means of these two very clear-cut ways: forgiveness and exclusion. Forgiveness means that the evil is removed through an inner change. Exclusion means that the evil is removed along with the person affected by it.

Rhön Bruderhof, Summer 1933

The authority to forgive sins, the lifting of the exclusion, the reacceptance into the bond of grace, the tangible reality of repentance and faith—all this is so unspeakably great that we can only stand before it in prayerful silence. (Matt. 18:18) The bond that unites us when faith enters our hearts is a gift we should treasure above all else. And my deepest longing is that faith be renewed in each one of us, that faith enter our hearts, that Christ be revealed in our midst and God's power can work freely.

Members' meeting, Rhön Bruderhof, Aug. 23, 1935

DISCIPLINE HAS TO BE VOLUNTARY

At times one of our circle comes to recognize with the others the necessity of seeking a deep inner silence in solitude for a time. This is never done unless the person concerned realizes the need for it and suggests it. He or she looks forward, with everyone else, to the joyful moment when this solitude bears fruit in a fuller and deeper fellowship.

Meeting with guests, Rhön Bruderhof, Aug. 14, 1935

When anyone talks about wanting to leave, all we can say is, go then! And no one can return until he or she is truly repentant and ready to admit it. Our life is entirely voluntary.

A man cannot tread this path for the sake of a girl he loves, nor can a wife do so for the sake of her beloved husband, nor parents for the sake of their children, nor children for the sake of their parents, nor friends for each other's sake. A voluntary life means that a person's will is set free for God and His Kingdom. This freedom of will leads to a free obedience born of faith and divine love. Then stubborn self-will is given up. That is why we welcome admonition. We submit to discipline and accept the need for times of quiet to consider our lives and cleanse our hearts of everything that comes from the evil spirit. (Prov. 3:11–12)

Members' meeting, Rhön Bruderhof, July 3, 1933

STRAIGHT TALKING IN LOVE

There is no law but that of love. (2 John 5–6) Love means having joy in others. Then what does being annoyed with them mean?

Words of love convey the joy we have in the presence of brothers and sisters. By the same token it is out of the question to speak about a Brotherhood member in a spirit of irritation or vexation. There must never be talk, either in open remarks or by insinuation, against a brother or a sister, against their individual characteristics—under no circumstances behind the person's back. Talking in one's own family is no exception.

Without this rule of silence there can be no loyalty, no community. Direct address is the only way possible; it is the spontaneous brotherly service we owe anyone whose weaknesses cause a negative reaction in us. An open word spoken directly to the other person deepens friendship and is not resented. Only when two people do not come to agreement quickly in this direct manner is it necessary to talk it over with a third person who can be trusted to help solve the difficulty and bring about a uniting on the highest and deepest levels. (Matt. 18:15–16)

Each one in the household should hang this reminder up where he works and can see it all the time.

"The First Law in Sannerz," 1925; English translation:
Foundation and Orders 1920–1929, *pp. 48–49*

Woe to us if we do the correct thing but have no love. Woe to us if we say the correct thing but have no love. (1 Cor. 13:1) Then it would be better to say nothing. Never tell a person an unpleasant truth unless the Holy Spirit has given you the assurance that you love that person with all your heart and you may therefore say it. (Eph. 4:15) Woe to anyone who admonishes brothers or sisters and does not have love for them in his heart. He is a murderer. For truth without love kills, while love without truth lies.

Worship meeting, Rhön Bruderhof, July 17, 1933

Jesus has this to say: When you live from the source you will speak up courageously; your words will be truthful, precise, clear, firm, and plain. You will not be evasive the minute you are told you have done something wrong. You will speak up and take on the guilt of what you have done. You will own up to what you are. You will admit honestly and simply to your own weaknesses and acknowledge God's strength. (1 Cor. 13:4–7) So you will be glad to reveal your weakness, for you no longer seek your own honor.

We can simply be ourselves, since we are not concerned with our own importance, but with God's honor, God's importance.

Rhön Bruderhof, Jan. 26, 1935

Love sees the good Spirit and the inner light at work in a person and delights in him. (Rom. 12:9–10) As soon as love rules in us again, we can feel new joy in someone with whom we have just been annoyed. We will overcome our personal disagreements to the degree that we joyfully acknowledge the working of the good Spirit in each other.

Augustine goes even further. He says we ought not to see each other as we are now; we should look at each other in love and each see the others as they are meant to be, to see them as they will be when God's Spirit fills them completely and makes them useful. (2 Cor. 5:16–17) When we take love's prophetic point of view, we see each other as something to be carved from wood that may still be too hard (or too soft), and we think of what God plans to make out of it.

Rhön Bruderhof, Mar. 20, 1933

The Individual in the Community

EACH INDIVIDUAL IS UNIQUE

What we have all been looking for is a life where brotherliness is voluntary, where there is no artificial attempt to make people equal, but where all are of equal worth and are therefore free to be very different. The more original an individual is, the better we like it. We have found that the greater the differences between people, the closer they may come to each other inwardly. We affirm the individual personality: each person, adult or child, is unique, and we educate all of them as individuals. But this uniqueness, taken to the ultimate depths, must lead us to the Church. If we all go into the depths, we will all be united. The more original and genuine we are, the more fully will we all be one.

Meeting with guests, Alm Bruderhof, July 2, 1935

Never push anyone in the area of faith and love. Wait patiently for God's hour for each person. These things need time to mature and unfold in God's way, and we must not act independently to interfere with His plan. One of the worst mistakes people in some religious circles make is to go blundering with their human will into the inner growth of something God is doing through Jesus. In each one of us this inner growth took time, and no human being had any business meddling or interfering with it. It needed to be clarified and illumined by God's light and purified by His fire. Then, when we were inwardly ready, we could accept Christ's truth, God's love, and the peace of His Kingdom.

Worship meeting, June 20, 1934

Moral coercion is excluded from the Church altogether. What is it? All coercion is pressure exerted by one person on another. God never uses coercion. There is no more evil opponent of God's word than human law. Jesus sharply opposed false prophecy and the Pharisees who represented it, and He leveled the reproach at them: You annul God's word with human commandments! (Matt. 15:6–9) The worst false prophet is one who wants to impose on others his own will, which is just as human as it is moralistic. Moral coercion has similar effects to physical violence, which, taken to extremes, is murder. In certain cases moral coercion is more destructive than physical violence. In its worst forms, it violates the whole life of a soul.

Novice meeting, Alm Bruderhof, Sept. 10, 1934

CALLED TO SERVE

It is not enough for Jesus that we set aside part of our strength for Him, even if it is a large part. He wants the whole of us. He is not satisfied if our religion is just a quest for inner peace and comfort. He wants us to dedicate ourselves totally to serve Him and work for Him. A so-called faith that does not show in our daily lives is of no use to Him.

God's clear demand is for our complete obedience in faith. We should go through fire and water to do what He says. So let us not fool ourselves! Our words and prayers, our church-going or attendance at meetings, our charity and philanthropy, will show that our life is lived in God only when our faith is genuine enough to make us hand ourselves over to God in resolute obedience. Deeds, not words and feelings, are the test of our faith. (Matt. 7:21)

Written for his fiancée,
Emmy von Hollander, June 6, 1907

Remember: the reason we live in community is not so that the individual members can attain the highest possible degree of perfection.

Instead, we believe that by living in total community we set an example and that this is the best service we can do for society today in its fragmented state. We want all those who sigh and groan under the wrongs in today's world to see that full community lived in love is possible!

There may be people who are not called just now to come and live in total community. They may feel a specific call to do a different kind of work to help humanity. And it is surely love that urges them to serve their fellows.

Meeting with guests, Rhön Bruderhof, Aug. 14, 1935

We certainly do not believe in people, we do not believe in the goodness of human beings. I do not believe in my goodness or your goodness. (Isa. 64:6; Rom. 3:23) Both good and evil are at work with immense force in every human being. This recognition is the only basis for mutual trust.

Meeting with guests, Rhön Bruderhof, Nov. 1932

It is so easy for us to think that the bond of faith consists only in our faithfulness. That is wrong. It is God's faithfulness that makes the bond. (Eph. 2:8)

The rock on which the Church was to be founded was not Peter himself, but his faith. Jesus said to Peter, in effect, "Your firm conduct was your own achievement. You were the one who made yourself firm and girded yourself. Now it will be Another who makes you firm and girds your loins—even for death. Follow me! Go my way." (John 21:18–19)

Members' meeting, Rhön Bruderhof, Oct. 14, 1935

We can never say we are strong in faith. That is impossible. When one grows in faith, one feels weak. (2 Cor. 12:9–10) It means that one hungers and thirsts for God's righteousness, which one does not have.

Rhön Bruderhof, July 24, 1932

In such dangerous times as these, we will only survive if each individual is inwardly awake and interested and ready to take an active part in the struggle, and that includes a personal interest in current world events. But for that to happen, our common life needs a deep and firm grounding in the order brought about by the Spirit. Then the personal or private concerns of individuals will recede into the background. Any personal striving for holiness will be given up for the sake of the greater cause; then, because it is given up, something new can be given. Self-abasing comparisons and feelings of inferiority simply vanish. Envy disappears, and so do selfish, touchy stubbornness and pride. No one can remain indifferent, weary, sluggish, sleepy, apathetic, or unmoved.

Worship meeting, Rhön Bruderhof, Nov. 21, 1934

INDIVIDUAL GIFTS

A person's natural gifts are, to begin with, neither a help nor a hindrance in this communal life. First of all, we need to become free, regardless of whether we are favored with gifts or not. We need to be liberated from the whole idea of this question, so liberated that there is absolutely no pride at all in being gifted and no feeling of inferiority about being less gifted. Instead, there will be exuberant joy in the grace of Jesus Christ, who has accepted each one just as he or she is.

Worship meeting, June 20, 1934

Whether people are very gifted or not so gifted, if they are freed from their selfish life, they can use all their physical and mental abilities to serve the community. They give what they have and do what they can. If we have much, we give much; if we have little, we give the little we have. Even those whose working strength is very limited do whatever they can. And those who are very capable and strong should likewise give all they can.

Meeting with guests, Rhön Bruderhof, Aug. 1933

We should be ready to spend several hours each day (provided we are in good health) doing physical work. Intellectuals, in particular, would discover the wholesome effect this has. Daily practical work allows each person's special little light, his or her special gift, to be kindled. This spark in each one, though maybe hidden, gives a glimpse of various gifts —possibly in scholarship, music, the use of words, creative art in woodwork, sculpture, or painting. Or simplest and best of all, a nature-loving person may have a particular gift for farm or garden work. And then, what people do in their spare time will show what gives them the most joy. So we can see to what extent readiness to help freewillingly to support the cause of love determines a person's whole life. Idleness and tedium are symptoms of death. Where there is life, people have alert, creative minds and are ready to serve and help one another.

This is not mere fantasy about an unattainable future; it is a present reality in a growing community.

Sannerz, 1921 or 1922

WHAT IS FREEDOM?

Early attempts at air travel began with a captive balloon. A gas-filled balloon tied to a steel cable was fastened to the ground. This symbolizes moral law, human tenets, and iron constraint. There is no free will in it. It is legalism, and that cannot exist in the Church of the Spirit.

Then people risked it to allow the gas-filled balloon to rise unhindered. They abandoned it to the winds and storms high in the atmosphere. Just as people often use the expression "free will" naively and thoughtlessly, they called this vessel a "free" balloon. Was it really free? Could its crew be called free when they were driven out over the ocean at the mercy of storms and thrown out of their airship so that they drowned, or were carried out over the desert where they crashed and died of the heat? That so-called freedom was really dangerous instability.

Imagine a young man walking down the streets of a big city. He is surrounded by brightly lit advertising. Movie theaters, music halls, cabarets, and taverns lure him. Women accost him. An excited political mob tries to incite him to murder. Impurity and bloodshed, lying and deceit surround him like winds blowing from all sides. Darkness settles over his heart. The true face of things is veiled. He succumbs to the great delusion of corrupt and uncontrolled life. If this young man suddenly decides to obey one of these winds, does that make him free? Was it his free will acting? He may say yes, and even if he regrets it later, he may still think that he did what he wanted to do. Possibly. No doubt he was free to do evil. But he was not free to do good when he did things that later caused him remorse. It certainly was will, but it was not free will. His will was just as badly enslaved and subjugated as the free balloon drifting out over sea or desert.

The modern airplane can picture for us what true freedom guided by the Spirit is. No matter which way the wind blows, the pilot flies his plane in the direction he decides. With this flight, all he has had in mind, all that has inspired his heart will be carried out. For thousands of years humankind has had this same ability to steer ships purposefully by the helm. When Christ is in the ship, it is steered by the Holy Spirit. The Elder represents Him at the helm. And if the entire crew and passengers look to no guidance but that of the good Spirit, then they are all truly free.

Novice meeting, Alm Bruderhof, Sept. 10, 1934

God's will is to take care of the most insignificant human being, and He waits for the least and lowliest to declare their readiness. He will not intervene in our lives unless we declare our readiness. For just as He made the atom, He made the tiny little human being as a diminutive created world that shall reveal the Creator in all His greatness. Therefore this being must have a free will and be able to use his powers freely. God does not want anything stiff, straightlaced, or hardened. He wants a free movement of heart. He wants us to act out of the innermost free will. The essence of His love to us consists in this very fact. His love would not contain even a spark of esteem for the mystery of human nature if He did not respect our free will. That is why He wants us to pray. But the human will is weak and fickle. We are not gods, we are men and women. We need to renew our readiness and to declare it over and over again. Therefore we need daily prayer. God wants to act. He is ready to intervene. He wants movement. And now He wants us to be ready and to declare our readiness.

Rhön Bruderhof, Jan. 27, 1935

PERSONAL PRAYER

People who spend all their energy on keeping their own salvation or their inner life above water are so preoccupied that they have no strength left to love. But people who are saved from the death of a separated, egocentric life are given a share in the power that streams from God's unity. They will devote this power to the One who freed them. Then they will love everybody, so that through God's unity a freeing is given to all those who are willing to receive the Word in Jesus. That is why the love to Jesus, this ardent personal love to God, who has shown His heart to us, is and always will be the living proof of unity in all areas of life. This love finds its living expression in the intimate, heart-to-heart relationship of prayer to the One we love.

1929; English translation: Prayer Life, *pp. 4–5.*

During this time I ask from the bottom of my heart that we, you and I, take time for personal prayer, each of us in the quiet of our own room or wherever we may be. (Matt. 6:6) Every morning on getting up and every night, our first and last thoughts should be of what is greatest in Heaven and earth. By bending the knees of our hearts and stretching out the hands of our souls, we will find this innermost recollection, in solitude or in the quiet gathering of two. Let us send up our prayer that everything that is to be given us in the time of Advent, everything that is to happen, may be made ready.

Perhaps it is best as it is done at the old Hutterian Bruderhofs, where each one kneels down by his window and lifts up his hands and turns to acknowledge his God in silent prayer. The prophet Daniel did this when he knelt down and turned his face toward the city of Jerusalem. Let us acknowledge God and praise Him and pray for the heavenly Jerusalem to come down to us. (Heb. 12:22)

Members' meeting, Rhön Bruderhof, Nov. 7, 1935

When we pray, we should not only bring our requests to God; we must be silent so we can hear what He is saying to us. God speaks to us through the word of the apostles and prophets, through the word of the early Church in Jerusalem. He speaks through the inner voice and the inner light in our hearts. He speaks through the power of the future world and the perfect justice which His Kingdom will bring over the whole earth.

Members' meeting, Rhön Bruderhof, July 9, 1933

Truthful and sincere prayer, the prayer of those whose daily practical life is at one with God's will, comes straight into God's presence. It reaches His heart, which has been waiting and longing for our human will to bend at last to His will. He answers us right away: Your prayer is heard! (1 John 5:14–15)

God is always at hand to listen to His people whenever their prayer is in accordance with His will. He is very close when we are so deep in trouble that we have stopped looking for help from our own efforts or from any human source. He is near, very near, when we pray for nothing but the honor of His name, when we ask for nothing but His intervention, His fire, His rain, the shining and streaming energy of His love.

1929; English translation: Prayer Life, *p. 22*

Each one of us has experienced that God is always ready to help, to save and heal, to give repentance and faith, to strengthen and renew our life.

But each one of us has also experienced that God does none of these things so long as we are halfhearted, so long as our soul is divided, so long as we are not honestly willing to let God rule supreme. When our will is not fully in accord with God's, He will never force His will on us. It is God's nature never to do violence to anyone.

Worship meeting, Rhön Bruderhof, Sept. 2, 1935

SOLITUDE AND FELLOWSHIP

Jesus looked for solitude. (Mark 1:35) He went up into the mountains or down to the quiet lake. Especially at night he sought to be alone so as to meet His God face to face. Before starting His ministry, He went into the loneliness of the desert for as long as forty days. (Luke 4:1-2) But he never remained alone. He stayed only long enough to receive strength to go back among people. Then He gathered His twelve disciples about Him, and they stayed together in a communal life of brotherhood. The purpose, however, was not so that Jesus could stay isolated with just these twelve. Their common life was meant to be a source of strength from which to go out to all people.

And in our communal life it is exactly the same. For a group of families (like the Bruderhof), as well as for each individual in the community, this rhythm or alternation is very important. Each person has to find the right balance between solitude and fellowship, that is to say, between encountering God alone and in the Brotherhood.

Meeting with guests, Rhön Bruderhof, Aug. 14, 1935

A NEW TOUCHSTONE FOR THE TRUTH

Is the evidence of our own heart all we are going to rely on for the truth? Or won't our hearts, appealed to at the deepest level, lead us to the same unity that the early Church experienced: They were all, yes all, united.

That question is important, also, for our understanding of the Bible. There are two very different positions on this question. One is that individuals are aware of their conscience, their inspiration, and their enlightenment. Out of this awareness they form their judgment on all things, and that includes the Bible.

The other position does not exclude the individual conscience, but its main feature is faith in the Spirit, who guides all who are of one accord into the same truth and the same love. (1 Cor. 1:10) That way a new touchstone for the truth is established, a new guideline of discernment.

Meeting with guests, Rhön Bruderhof, Nov. 6, 1935

Marriage and Family

MARRIAGE IS HOLY

Matrimony is a sacrament. (Mark 10:7–9) A sacrament is a holy act that helps us understand a basic reality, for instance, the Lord's Supper or baptism. Our whole life is a sacrament, giving visible form to a basic reality.

Worship meeting, Alm Bruderhof, Aug. 23, 1934

The unity and purity in marriage as taught by Jesus and His apostles are unique. They have nothing to do with the old nature. They belong to the new Church order, which as brotherly justice lets the Spirit of love rule supreme. Unity and purity in marriage do not belong to unredeemed human nature. They can be realized only in the new Church of the Spirit of Jesus Christ. They belong to the Kingdom of God. They are symbol and sacrament of that Kingdom.

Inner Land, p. 156

Marriage is a mystery. The Apostle Paul says, "When I speak of this mystery, I speak of Christ and the Church." (Eph. 5:31–32) To Paul the Church is something hidden. The

Church does not throw holy things to the dogs. It does not expose itself. Its members do proclaim the Gospel to those outside, and this is as it should be. But the Church itself remains hidden for the great day. For it is the one Church of the one Bridegroom, kept for Him. (Rev. 19:7)

In the same way, every human being should keep his or her body pure for marriage, which symbolizes the unity of Christ with His Church. Marriage reveals the divine mystery that the spiritual unity of two, when their hearts vibrate as one, leads to their physical uniting. Two become one and their unity contains the creative power of birth, for in the physical realm of procreation the powers of God's whole creation are shown.

Rhön Bruderhof, July 8, 1934

THE RIGHT FOUNDATION

Much of what people call love is nothing but selfish desire. It is an improvement over individual selfishness when people decide not to go on living alone but to live selfishly together as a couple: Fénelon calls it "égoïsme à deux" (selfishness together).* It is better yet if these two people live for their children and grandchildren, but we should realize that this is still collective egoism. If we think of the sacrifices people make for their country, we have to admit that this again is a higher form of love; yet class and national collectivism is merely a merging of many egoisms in a collective egoism. All these can be called love: love of family, group solidarity, patriotism. God's love is more than all these.

The fellowship founded by God in Christ does not originate in the egoism of individuals or groups. The Bruderhof

---

*François de Fénelon, French theologian, 1651–1715.

does not exist for the Bruderhof's sake. We are not concerned with communal life for its own sake. God's heart—the unity that springs from His love—is what counts. In Christ, God has revealed His heart.

Meeting with guests, Alm Bruderhof, Aug. 2, 1934
(This and other extracts in this chapter
are from Love and Marriage in the Spirit)

Being united in faith is the only foundation on which life —and that means marriage too—can be built up. From this it is plain that also in marriage the issue is not marriage as such, but unity in God's Kingdom, unity in Christ and His Holy Spirit. We are reminded of Jesus' words, "Strive first for the Kingdom of God and His justice, and everything else shall be given to you." (Matt. 6:33) That includes marrying or not marrying. Marriage is only one example from actual life; the same is true of every other area.

Worship meeting, Alm Bruderhof, Aug. 24, 1934

There can be no remarriage on the basis of divorce or separation. (Luke 16:18) What is joined together on earth in the unity of the Spirit is joined together in Eternity. So long as both partners are living, nothing can alter this fact. (Matt. 19:3–6) Not even the unfaithfulness of one partner can change anything; that does not give the innocent partner the freedom to enter a second marriage while the other partner is living. Because the unity of the Church is eternal and unchangeable, marriage too has to be indissoluble.

Alm Bruderhof, June 9, 1934

God's economy, His plan for the household of His Church through the ages, requires that all unclear human relationships are set in order. Debts or promises, financial commitments of any kind—all these things have to be settled. Similarly, in all matters pertaining to marriage there has to be complete clarity.

Members' meeting, Rhön Bruderhof, July 3, 1933

HUSBAND AND WIFE

The claim that love is nothing but an episode in a person's life is true only of superficial relationships based on physical attraction. These lack the deeper communion of soul and spirit. Partners whose love springs from common spiritual concerns, whose hearts beat together, will increasingly support and encourage each other. Such love can never end, because it originates in the eternal Spirit and does not depend on physical and emotional states.

Essay, Sannerz, 1920

The times we live in are extremely difficult, and many people live in great need. To form a marriage bond in such times is a step in faith. Faith is courage; there is no fear in it. We do not know what the future holds for any of us—it may well be that a few of us or many of us will have to suffer a violent death, and it is possible that some married couples will be suddenly torn apart. So we rejoice all the more when two young people are led together and we can state: Come what may, they are a married couple. In today's world it is essential that here and there rays of light and hope continue to shine, spiritual realities that demonstrate the unity of God's peace, true brotherliness, and justice.

Wedding meeting, Alm Bruderhof, May 19, 1935

We need to ask God that in all our marriages in the Church we fulfill His divine order. In this divine order there can be no tyrannizing by men or by women, neither in the Church nor in any marriage in the Church. It should be out of the question for one spouse to keep on nagging the other; that would make anyone gradually lose confidence and efficiency. It is the husband's duty to head the family, to guide the family to unity and perfect clarity. (Eph. 5:21–28) If anyone thinks that a certain wife is born to lead her family and that her husband's natural tendency is to follow her, he is mistaken. That is not true, not in any family; it is simply against nature. The consequences will be felt in the Church. It robs the husband of any capacity to do a service in the Church; it weighs on him and squeezes the life out of him. *And the outcome would be the same if the husband tyrannized his wife;* if instead of heading the family by serving, he lorded it over his wife and kept her under his thumb. The result would be equally crushing and destructive. (Col. 3:19; 1 Pet. 3:7)

Worship meeting, Alm Bruderhof, June 14, 1934
(Cf. "Christ the Head," in Love and Marriage*)*

Woman is called to a way of love that is not given to man. A man seeks people out at the moment when he knows they need a challenge, when he realizes that a person needs to be shaken and awakened and convinced. A woman is quite different. Her love is steady, faithful, constant. Her motherly and sisterly help goes to those already close to her more naturally than to strangers and newcomers, whereas a man will direct his energies most of all to strangers and newcomers.

Of course, not every man has received the same gifts. But we feel that any kind of work is an expression of love. Men have greater muscular strength and ability to take the initiative in the world around them. They are competent in leading a battle, in governing, in steering the ship of war. The man's gifts are not worth more; they are simply different.

The kind of work that falls to woman does not usually demand great physical strength. It is more in keeping with her loving, loyal, quiet nature. Woman's role is to be loving and motherly, to dedicate herself to protecting, preserving, and keeping pure her family circle and all those in her care; to train, foster, and care for them. A woman may be active in different spheres—intellectual, cultural, practical, or any others; that will vary a great deal. But if she remains a true woman, her caring love for those entrusted to her will always be present, whatever she does. (Prov. 31:10–31)

Man's work, the struggle and pioneering and conflict with the world outside, is under no circumstances to be more highly prized than this inward and creative giving of life and depth to the Church community. It is not a matter of different values; it is the calling that is different.

Alm Bruderhof, late Summer 1934

Christ is Head of the Church; He is the Word in all its clarity; He is the true direction. The Elder or Shepherd has to represent the Word, that is, Christ. And in marriage the husband has to do the same. That is why we say that the husband is the head of his wife. He is the head, though not in himself but in Christ. (1 Cor. 11:1–3) This should not be taken to mean that the husband is literally an overlord. Unless this is understood in its deeper, inner meaning, in the Spirit, the results will be disastrous. But in the Church, if it is led by the Holy Spirit alone, something God-given will come of it. It will give Christ His true place.

Alm Bruderhof, Sept. 1935

In our history there have been cases where only one partner of a married couple belonged to the life and faith of the Church community. This partner was a member, living and working with full responsibility in the community. The other partner was not a member, not even a novice member. Since they wished to live together in matrimony (a situation such as Paul writes about in his First Letter to the Corinthians, 1 Cor. 7:12–16), it was arranged to have the family live on the edge of the community land. One partner spent the day at the community, the other outside it. According to Paul, this attempt should be made as long as the partner who does not share the faith and life of the Church gladly allows the other to give all his or her strength to the Church and God's Kingdom.

Rhön Bruderhof, Feb. 1933

REVERENCE FOR LIFE

Countless people today have no qualms of conscience when souls are crushed by unfaithfulness; nor does it trouble them when the life of tiny beings is prevented or annihilated.

Souls wait in vain to be called out of Eternity. Living human souls wait in vain to be called by constancy and faithfulness. There seems to be an ever smaller circle of people whose consciences protest clearly when the creative Spirit is scorned in this way and when the longing for unity, faithfulness, and constancy is despised.

Inner Land, pp. 138–139

Moral philosophers may demand that the sexual life be purified by insisting on purity before and in marriage. But even the best of them are insincere and unjust unless they clearly state the actual basis for such high demands. Even the destruction of incipient life—a Massacre of the Innocents intensified a thousandfold today—remains unassailable when people do not believe in the Kingdom of God. The supposedly high culture of our day will continue to practice this massacre as long as social disorder and injustice last. Infant murder cannot be combated as long as private and public life are allowed to continue as before.

If we want to fight acquisitiveness and the deceit and injustice of social distinctions, we must fight them in a practical way by demonstrating that a different way of life is not only feasible but actually exists. Otherwise we can demand neither purity in marriage nor an end to infant murder; we cannot wish even the finest families to be blessed with the many children intended by God's creative powers. Christian marriage cannot be demanded of anyone outside the whole context of life represented in the words "Kingdom of God" and "Church of Jesus Christ."

Inner Land, p. 155

In our families we hope for as many children as God gives. We praise God's creative power and welcome large families as one of His great gifts. It is our hope that family life among us will always be firmly established in the framework of our communal life and work. . . .

THE FAMILY AND COMMUNAL LIFE

Families are founded within the framework of the community. We keep strict discipline in our family life, and our young people stay away from anything that could stain a later marriage. They live in complete purity and abstinence. The only marriage we recognize is that of one man with one woman.

Family life does not suffer from the communal life and activity. On the contrary, the joy of a married couple in each other and in their children is especially strong and deep. This is because the entire education of our children is placed under the Spirit of the Church community.

Meeting with guests, Rhön Bruderhof, July 16, 1933

God is at the root and core of a life where creative love is evident in working together. As long as any circle is truly alive for God, there can be no question of permanent withdrawal or isolation from the world. The life of a family or group of families is healthy and strong only as long as its members direct their activity outward and seek fellowship with other people too. Historically the family has always been the nuclear cell of a people, the cradle of their strength. All the more, any communal group of families held together by the true Spirit will surely have an impact upon society at large.

"Familienverband und Siedlungsleben,"
Das neue Werk, *1920*

THE UNMARRIED

Now some may ask about those who can never find the happiness of unity between two in body, soul, and spirit; here we stand before the mystery of a most noble calling of God's love. When people are deeply unhappy in their disappointed or frustrated desires, it needs an impulse from the world of the eternal powers before they can arrive at a decision that makes them completely happy. Those who long for the garden of love when it is closed to them, who rattle its locked gates, cannot find this secret. . . .

There is a complete freeing from the eros of selfish desire

when eros is wedded in everlasting faithfulness to agape. Those who can be liberated once and for all from the sexual belong to the happiest of people. They are able to love more than all others because their entire time and strength are free, because agape, God's love, dominates exclusively their relationships to all men and women. Through them the heavenly Kingdom can break in upon earth more freely because all the threads of their love run in one single direction. In this sense Jesus spoke of those who are eunuchs for the sake of the Kingdom of Heaven (Matt. 19:12), and Paul spoke of those for whom it is better to stay unmarried because their special calling requires them to be specially equipped. (1 Cor. 7)

Men and women for whom the way to the one pure marriage seems to be closed must not become embittered and withdrawn from life and love. They must not stifle the best in themselves. They must never yield to appetites that prevent the awakening and unfolding of what is best in them, above all, what is of God in them. Instead, they have received the higher calling, in which all their powers of love are kindled and revived by the generous, sunny love of God. Their powers of love are not spent in possessive desire but exclusively in enthusiastic lavish giving. Then, love to many, to all, takes over —love that wants nothing for itself but is fulfilled in giving.

"Liebesleben und Liebe," Junge Saat:
Lebensbuch einer Jugendbewegung, *1920*

WHO IS MY MOTHER?
WHO ARE MY BROTHERS?

The fulfillment of the Ten Commandments, including the commandment to honor father and mother, consists in living a life of love and unbroken unity. A person can do no better service to parents, brother or sister, wife or husband, or children, than to lead them to such a life and to call others to go this way.

It is in connection with this commandment that the relationship between Jesus and His mother is often brought into the picture. The Gospels mention four episodes, four confrontations between Jesus and His mother. First when He was still a boy. (Luke 2:41–51) As a twelve-year-old He left His father and mother and went to the house of God to read, study, and represent the truth. When He had fulfilled that task, He returned to His parents (who had been anxiously looking for Him) and from then on was obedient to them as befitted a child of His age. This was the first break the future Savior of the world made. It placed Him in such serious opposition to His parents that His mother asked Him, "My son, why have you treated us like this?" At the same time we can see that Jesus (who was truly human and grew up like any other boy) was neither forward nor precocious. After this first break, He took His place in His parental home like any other child His age.

The second confrontation was at the wedding in Cana. (John 2:1–11) Jesus had just begun His public activity. The first remarkable deed of His to be recorded took place at this celebration of unity; that was the time He chose to reveal the glory of God on the ground of the first creation. This time the conflict between Jesus and His mother was more obvious than when He was twelve. Mary, His mother, believed she still had authority over Him; she wanted to give Him advice and expected Him to follow it. His answer was sharp: "Woman, what have I to do with you? My hour is not yet come." His mother was not the one to determine the hour; that had to come directly from God. And then Jesus did even more than she had expected.

In the third encounter the conflict is intensified yet more. Jesus, facing a crowd of people, is proving to them the decisive power of God's Kingdom over their bodies and souls. His mother and brothers, standing at the edge of the crowd, think He has lost His wits. They send Him a message to go home to His mother, and Jesus sends back the answer: "Who is my mother? Who are my brothers?" (Matt. 12:46–50) You, Mary, are not my mother; you other sons of Mary are not my brothers unless you do God's will. The Church of those who do the will of God is my mother, and my brothers are those with whom I am in unity, who do the will of my Father.

All the threads that had apparently been broken by these shaking confrontations were drawn together again in a final unity. That was the fourth encounter. When Jesus was put to death, His mother and His beloved disciple John stood at the foot of the gallows, the Cross. And He told His mother and His beloved disciple to take care of each other. (John 19:25–27) He united His disciples, those who did His will, with His mother, who from that moment on also wanted to do His will. So we find His mother, who had previously seemed to separate herself from Him, waiting with all the others for the outpouring of the Holy Spirit and for the creation of the first communal Church at Pentecost. From then on she belonged fully to the circle of those who believed in her Son. (Acts 1:14)

Rhön Bruderhof, Jan. 13, 1933

Education *

The Bruderhof is an educational community, both humanly seen and in the sense that every one of us has to be taught by God. That process is never finished.

It is mainly a matter of awakening the inner life, of quickening it so that we are filled with enthusiasm for the Holy Spirit and for deep, living experiences. Then we will all learn to put the great things above the small and to go forward giving every ounce of strength.

Members' meeting, Rhön Bruderhof, Dec. 4, 1932

How can we bring up our children now so that they become courageous fighters in faith and brave martyrs for Christ? How can we bring up our children to feel straightaway that they are being given to God? Children are not possessions; from the first breath they draw we consecrate them to the great cause of the future. They are consecrated to God even before they are born and after they are born, especially in the first years of life. Just then it is very important to guide their instincts in such a way that they do not pursue their own

---

*For this chapter extensive use has been made of Eberhard Arnold, *Children's Education in Community.*

pleasure but from an early age are encouraged to overcome themselves and give themselves to the cause.

Members' meeting, Rhön Bruderhof, Sept. 20, 1935

The only true service to our children is to help them become what they already are in God's thoughts. Each child is a thought in the mind of God. We must not try to form a child according to our own ideas for his or her life. That would not be a true service. The only way we can do that service is to understand in each one the thought God has had for that child from all Eternity, and still has and will always have. (Ps. 139:13–17)

Worship meeting, Alm Bruderhof, Sept. 30, 1934

THE CHILDLIKE SPIRIT AND FREEDOM

Genuine children will tell us immediately what they feel. As long as we let them be children, they will tell us about anything they do not like. They will not be silent about something to a person's face and then talk about it behind his back. Cowardly deception is unchildlike. True children are completely open; they are always ready to tell us whatever is in their hearts. . . .

One of the sternest things Jesus ever said was: "If anyone corrupts one of these little children"—so that he can no longer be a child—"it would be better for him to be drowned with a millstone around his neck." It would really be better for him not to live. "Woe to the man by whom offenses come. If your hand or foot offends you, chop off that member and throw it away. If your eye entices you to evil, pluck it out and throw it away. Watch that you do not hold little children in contempt, for I tell you that their angels always have access to my Father." (Matt. 18:6–10)

Remarkable words! How infinitely deep was the insight that set these words (about cutting off hand or foot and tearing out an eye) next to the words about children. It is better for a Church to have the all-seeing eye torn out or the efficient hand cut off than for a child to lose his childlike spirit. It would be better for anyone who corrupts a child not to live.

That is corruption—to rob anyone of the childlike spirit. Anything that puts an end to childhood is corruption. That is why Jesus warns us to hold nothing in higher regard than children, to love nothing more deeply than the childlike spirit, to long for nothing else but to become like children, and never to look down on a child. You look down on children if you turn them into emotional parasites clinging to father or mother or some other person. You despise children not only by misleading them to sin but by anything you do that deprives them of their childlikeness. You have lost your reverence for the childlike nature of children the minute you try to make them your emotional property. Children are free, truly free. All children are free! They must never become the property of father or mother, much less of anyone else.

Worship meeting, Rhön Bruderhof, Oct. 13, 1935

Every genuine child wants to be daring and brave. Therefore, where relationships are built on trust between grown-ups and children, there will be as little restriction as possible on things like climbing trees, harnessing, riding, and grooming horses, and facing danger courageously.

In this freedom lies the best protection. Overprotection by anxious adults will not keep a child safe. Leading the child to acquire a sure instinct in dangerous situations, ultimately trusting in a care beyond our own power, is what gives true protection.

"Unser Weg zur Erziehung," Die Wegwarte, *April 1927*

GOOD AND EVIL IN CHILDREN

While our children are still at the innocent age when they are not yet fully awakened to good and evil and cannot yet discern between the two, our prayer should be that the whole atmosphere around them be filled with the Holy Spirit of purity and love. If that is not our main concern, we will be doing our children a great wrong. Later, when these children are slowly awaking, when they begin to discern between good and evil and to make their own decisions, we must pray for the Spirit of God to invade their souls and make their wills pure, clear, and decided.

Members' meeting, Rhön Bruderhof, Jan. 8, 1933

Children cease to be children the moment they consciously and willfully do evil. . . .

We adults are not capable of recognizing the moment when a young child first makes a conscious decision to do something wrong.

This admission ought to keep us from the bad practice of trying to catch children doing something wrong and punishing them then and there. If you distrust children and read bad motives into their actions, you weaken them instead of strengthening them. To force children to be aware of their bad impulses cannot be the healthy way. Any such attempt harms their inner life; it is cruel because it imputes bad will to the children. This kind of moral violence corrupts children's sense of good and bad, and no one has a right to do that. It is based on the false assumption that the evil will is fully developed in children. It is the educator—the parent or the teacher—whose will is evil, not the children. The odds are a hundred to one that when children do something bad, they do not do it with anything like the degree of consciousness that adults assume, accustomed as they are to deliberate evil.

"Der Kampf um die Kindheit,"
Die Wegwarte, *June/Sept. 1928*

AUTHORITY AND SELF-DISCIPLINE

The question of authority is crucial in bringing up children. The Bruderhof rejects these two extremes: authority based on physical force or on the power of suggestion; and a weak, blind lack of authority. Freedom for individual children and for the children's group does not mean that a child can follow every mood and every whim without restraint. Nor does the teachers' authority consist in imposing their own will on the children. Teachers should stimulate and awaken the children's discernment and the ability to make their own decisions for the good. Least of all should a teacher take harsh measures to force his or her will on helpless children for the sake of convenience or because of hurt pride. And yet it would be equally wrong for teachers not to exercise any leadership and just wait for the good to take over of its own accord and conquer the evil in the children or the group.

No; guidance is necessary. It is the greatest love we can show children. Children want to be guided, helped, and given direction, but they do not want to be coerced or crushed. (Col. 3:20–21) True authority combines with the unfolding of the best kind of freedom in the children, with the result that the teachers stimulate and strengthen what is good in the children and lead them to making their own decisions for the good. The children then feel the urge to fight and overcome the evil that also tries to work in them. The Bruderhof is convinced that humankind's greatest Leader spoke the decisive words in this area too when He said, "Let the children come to me, and do not stop them. Unless you become like these children, you cannot enter the Kingdom of God." (Luke 18:16–17)

Jesus showed us that we must lead children by trusting them and loving them. That is why He embraced and kissed them.

Pädagogische Warte, *Aug. 15, 1932*

Being firm and decisive helps children to fight against themselves much more than talking with them gently and patiently—too patiently—about their naughtiness. . . .

Corporal punishment is a declaration of bankruptcy. By resorting to corporal punishment we admit our failure to provide the spiritual and truly educational influence for our children. Simply because we, the educators, are imperfect and poor in spiritual gifts, we cannot always avoid a certain use of force. But it should be kept to the very minimum through the influence of the Spirit working in both educators and children. In its brutal forms corporal punishment can have no place in our education.

"Unser Weg zur Erziehung," Die Wegwarte, *April 1927*

It is important not to get into the habit of being too lenient with children's moods, either at home or in the children's groups. Children must learn to take themselves in hand. They must learn to take a firm stand to what they have done and to state it in a few words. They must not feel ill-used if someone has to speak sharply to them. They must learn to face up to what has happened when they are shown to be in the wrong and not give half-answers that could mean this or could mean that. They must learn to be brave and to speak up firmly and clearly.

Members' meeting, Rhön Bruderhof, Jan. 5, 1933

Children who are too good are a most unpleasant phenomenon because their good behavior is unnatural, forced, and hypocritical. But naughty children who are unchildlike, presumptuous, disrespectful, and impertinent are just as unpleasant. The same thing applies to all self-centeredness in petty quarrels or clamoring for some privilege or possession that is supposedly marvelous but actually silly. Another aspect of this evil is the chronic indifference and callous ingratitude that some children display toward the love and the good things they receive, often at great sacrifice.

Letter, 1934

CHILDREN AND EDUCATORS
IN A GREATER UNITY

Our nursery school is a tremendous gift from God. Here even the first child in a marriage cannot get his or her own way when he or she is greedy, possessive, or thinking just of himself or herself. Instead, this only child gets used to being part of a large group of children. When I was a boy of seven, my older brother asked me whether I had ever thought how good it was that we had five children in our family. He said he knew a family where there was only one child, and because that child had grown up alone, he wasn't a true child. When children are together in a large group, they cannot simply get their own way. They are part of a larger unit. The reason the children's community is of such crucial importance is that no one child is the center of attention. No child must be allowed to think even for a moment that everything revolves around him or her.

Members' meeting, Rhön Bruderhof, Sept. 20, 1935

All members of the community have an overwhelming responsibility that can be expressed in the words: reverence for the Holy Spirit. This applies to all parts of the Church, but in an especially holy sense it applies to the upbringing of children: reverence for father and mother—the father, whom God has placed at the head of the family and who, as bearer of the Spirit, must reflect Christ; the mother, who like Mary and the Church should also reflect Christ; reverence for the child, for the wonder and mystery of childhood and of becoming like a child; reverence for the spirit that lives and moves between parents and children; reverence for the Church and its services, which is reverence for the Holy Spirit who fills the whole Church.

Worship meeting, Alm Bruderhof, Sept. 30, 1934

How difficult it is for us human beings, who are not free of sin, to bring up children. What a responsibility! Only saints and the wise are fit to be educators. Our lips are unclean. Our surrender is not without reservation. Our truthfulness is broken. Our love is not perfect. Our kindness is not disinterested. We are not free of lovelessness, possessiveness, and selfishness. We are unjust.

It is the child who leads us to the Gospel. If we consider how holy is our task with the children, it is quite clear that we are too sinful to bring up even one single child. This recognition leads us to grace. Without the atmosphere of grace no one

can work with children. Only one who stands like a child before God can educate children, can live with children.

"You must become like children." (Matt. 18:3) Like children, we must live in the presence of grace. We must learn
wonder. In the knowledge of our own smallness, we marvel at
the greatness of the divine mystery that lies hidden in all
things and behind all things. Only then can we be given the
vision of this mystery. That vision makes us forget ourselves
because it overwhelms us with the greatness of the cause. Only
those who look with the eyes of children can lose themselves
in the object of their wonder.

"Der Kampf um die Kindheit,"
Die Wegwarte, *June/Sept. 1928*

It is very important for every educator to place equal val-
ue on all the abilities of mind and body and all the services
they render. As early as possible we must find out whether a
child is gifted more in physical work or more in mental activity, and what kind of achievement can be expected. If each
child is to develop his or her abilities freely, we must from the
very start dispel the illusion that some occupations are more
valuable than others. In fact they all are equally useful for the
common good. . . .

We do not teach religion as a specialized area of doctrine
and religious customs. Instead, starting with the reality and
working of the living God, the children are led to a religious
understanding of all areas of life. . . .

With good teaching the Spirit will be seen in the history
of religion as well as in arts and crafts, social studies, and in all
of nature and history. . . .

With this approach to learning, children discover Christ
everywhere. He comes close to them as the One who fulfills

the longing of humankind's religions through all ages, in all cultures, and on all continents. This brings to life the religious significance of history and opens up the Bible to the children.

"Unser Weg zur Erziehung,"
Die Wegwarte, *Apr. 1927*

Living Naturally

In 1899 and the following years, the youth movement sprang up in different parts of Germany. We young people had barely emerged from childhood. We longed to get out of the untruthful conditions in churches and schools. The fight for purity and freedom took different forms in different places, yet was the same fight. We were driven by the longing to live as natural human beings, to live with nature.

The whole rigid system of tradition and class distinction seemed to us an enslavement of true humanity. We wanted to get away from our social surroundings to the highways, fields, woods, and mountains. We fled the cities as much as possible. What were we looking for in nature? Freedom, friendship, community. We went out together, not isolated like hermits. Together we sought life in the outdoors.

Public lecture, Nov. 28, 1922

Postwar youth abhorred the big cities as places of impurity for body and soul. They felt the cities were seats of mammon; they felt the coldness and the poisonous air. They found that people did not live as God wants them to live. Families had two children, one child, or in many cases none. The whole atmosphere of the city seemed to them saturated with murder and degeneracy. The cities were straying far from what God wanted for human beings. So the young people left the cities. It was not quite the same as Rousseau's back-to-nature philosophy, but somewhat similar. They wanted to return to places where they could be close to God's creation, where they could feel afresh that God breathed His own living breath into human beings and into plants and animals. They wanted to get away from the stench, the dirt, and the smoke, and from the folly of human works.

Their spirit drew them back to nature, to ally themselves with the spirit at work there. To them the spirit at work in nature and the Spirit of God were one and the same. God first created the land and the plants and animals, and then He created man. They all were in harmony. In this movement [the youth movement] all of these flowed together again.

Public lecture, State University of
South Dakota, Apr. 21, 1931

To be simple, to be genuine, to have nothing to do with anything forced, unnatural, or artificial—these things have been of consuming importance to us from the very beginning of our life together. We wanted to live close to creation and nature. We longed to be so natural in our belief in God and in our understanding of His creation that no religious influence of any kind would be able to divert us from a childlike and simple way of living.

We realized that life in Church community is not possible unless it is completely natural. We knew that the common life would be lost if it were lulled into some form of artificial piety, if we were to adopt a language full of pious words that did not spring from deep roots, did not come genuinely from our hearts.

As with language, so it is with everything else. One legacy of the youth movement is our attitude to nature. It was not just romanticism that made us rejoice in meadows and flowers, woods and mountains. To experience nature helped us to come closer to the beginnings, to creation itself. We would have nothing to do with anything that did not spring straight from the inmost source.

Now it is my sincere longing that our common life spring directly from the ground of the heart, just as it is given to each one of us; that all false piety, all hypocrisy, be ruled out and what is natural be allowed to grow. We ask God to grant us a life full of this inner vitality, as alive as the plants, the stars, and the animals; as full of vitality as the birth and development of a child. May this be given in the life of each one of us. Then we shall know true faithfulness.

We should appreciate work on the land, especially in farm and garden, because of its closeness to nature, its intrinsic genuineness. It provides us with our daily food from God's hand, which gives us strength to cope with all that the heart and mind are called to do.

Worship meeting, Rhön Bruderhof, Mar. 24, 1935

When we left the State Churches, that did not mean that we broke with our Christian faith. It did mean that we broke away from a mode of life that was not in keeping with our faith.

Our reluctance to use the holiest word, the Name of the all-great and all-powerful Being, is a good thing. We do not wish to use this Name unnecessarily; we use it as seldom as possible. True, we are called to testify to this Name, but not in a way that casts pearls to the swine. (Matt. 7:6)

Mealtime at the Rhön Bruderhof, Jan. 30, 1933

Humanity will never renounce the longing to live in heartfelt love for one another in a new and richer Paradise. To delight in nature, to work with nature, to protect and deepen one's inner life, to experience God's nearness, and to be creative in works of love—these things are uppermost in every person's longing.

"Jesus und der Zukunftsstaat,"
unpublished article, 1919

People told us, "You are nature lovers, you want to go back to nature!" No, that was not what we wanted. On the contrary, we recognized more and more how badly corrupted nature is in the old creation. (Rom. 8:20–22) We did not want to return to the old nature (that is why we have always rejected nudism), but we did feel that behind nature the divine is at work. (Rom. 1:20; Ps. 19:1–4) Behind all nature we felt its inner coherence, its unity willed by God, in spite of the opposition of satanic and demonic forces. God's love is manifest in that unity. Creative life from God is revealed. What we worship is not things, not nature, but the mystery of God the Creator.

Rhön Bruderhof, May 12, 1935

That was also a danger in the youth movement. Some people revered creation itself. They romanticized the beauties of nature and of the human body. In some cases this led to nature worship. The next step was to reject the Creator in favor of the creature, just as National Socialism does today.

Worship meeting, Alm Bruderhof, June 2, 1935

In nature, too, there are good and evil side by side, light and shadow. Nature does not give us pure light but an alternation of light and darkness. Human life has its bright hours and its dark hours. So there has to be a revelation outside the book of nature. The book of nature is important, but it is not enough. The best advice for a person who does not yet believe in Jesus is to search the history of the human race for the person in whom God's truth and light are most clearly revealed. We recognize Jesus Christ to be that person. (Col. 1:15–20) We know that in Him there is nothing but light, that His love and His word give us perfect light, and that this light is indeed love. So we have come to know God as love. God is love; and he who remains in love remains in God and God in him. (1 John 4:15–16)

Meeting with guests, Rhön Bruderhof, Aug. 23, 1935

PEACE
AND THE RULE OF GOD

Folk dancing at the Alm Bruderhof, Liechtenstein, 1934

Non-Violence and
Refusal to Bear Arms

WHAT DOES THE GOSPEL SAY?

"Thou shalt not kill" was said to men of old. Jesus goes
further and says that words spoken in hate are like poisonous
knife stabs. Whoever denies that a fellow human has equal
rights is a murderer in the eyes of Jesus. And anyone who goes
to war acts against the words: "Love your enemies." (Matt.
5:43–48)

Meeting with guests, Rhön Bruderhof, Dec. 1932

Before Jesus died, He said He would be delivered into the
hands of those in authority: the pious, and the State. He would
have to surrender, defenseless, to their power. And when His
disciples asked, "Couldn't we call down the powers at our dis-
posal? We could make fire come down from heaven, we could
make lightning come down from the clouds," Jesus answered,
"Do you not know which spirit you belong to?" (Luke
9:54–55) You have forgotten the Spirit! You have forgotten
the cause, you have forgotten your highest calling. You leave
the Spirit the moment you take up the cause of force instead

of love, even if you call upon heavenly fire and heavenly lightning and heavenly miracles.

Rhön Bruderhof, Oct. 1931

In the name of Jesus Christ we can die, but not kill. This
is where the Gospel leads us. If we really want to follow
Christ, we must live as He lived and died. But this will not be
clear to us until we understand how final His words are: You
cannot serve God and mammon.

Meeting with guests, Rhön Bruderhof, Dec. 1932

The theological nonsense that came out there [at Tübing-
en University] was almost unbearable. A pious young woman
(a theology student) stood up and said, "Jesus said, I have not
come to bring peace, but the sword." (Matt. 10:34) I answered,
"I am very much surprised to hear these words in this context.
I don't understand what you mean. Jesus is talking about the
relationship between a daughter-in-law who wants to follow
Him and her mother-in-law who has not chosen the way of
discipleship. Are you trying to say that Jesus meant the daughter-in-law should kill her mother-in-law?"

Report about lecture at Tübingen,
Rhön Bruderhof, February 22, 1933

No one who has heard the clear call of Jesus' Spirit can
resort to violence for protection. Jesus abandoned every privilege and every defense. (1 Pet. 2:21–23) He took the lowliest
path. And that is His challenge to us: to follow Him on the
same way that He went, never departing from it either to the
left or to the right. Do you really think you can go a different

way from Jesus on such decisive points as property and violence and yet claim to be His disciple?

Rhön Bruderhof, Oct. 1931

LOVE YOUR ENEMIES

We could have reacted in either of two ways [to the armed robbery of two brothers], both of which would have been a betrayal of the cause. One extreme would have been to use force, which would have happened if the brothers had defended themselves with a stick, or if afterwards we had called the police or the civil authorities and given the power into their hands. The other extreme would have been to think we must protect the culprits from the clutches of the authorities, which would have meant that we supported the crime. Instead, we called a public meeting with all the carpenters and other workers [to lay the matter open], so that we did not become guilty of condoning the crime.

We have to raise a strong protest against this armed robbery. The Church of God is bound to protest publicly against any injustice. This incident must serve as an example by which to proclaim the Gospel of the Kingdom and witness to the justice of the Church, to brotherliness, to the love of enemies.

Members' meeting, Rhön Bruderhof, Oct. 25, 1931, after
two members, coming home from the local bank, had been
robbed at gunpoint of the week's wages for the
Bruderhof-employed carpenters and workmen

It is true that at the moment any person hits another, he is unable to see anything good in that person, or at least very little. We also know that from wartime. The war spirit has to be fanned by exaggeration and lying so that each nation will see as little good in the other as possible. Jesus could never fall for such deception. In each person He saw the image of God, imperfect and often distorted, yet truly an image of God in every human being. (Gen. 1:27)

Members' meeting, Rhön Bruderhof, June 14, 1932

How are we to take up this fight? In the Spirit of the coming Kingdom, and in no other way. We must fight this battle in love. The weapon of love is the only one we have. And whether we are confronted with a mounted policeman or someone in the Labor Service, whether we come into contact with a district president, a prince, a party leader, or even with the President of the Reich, it makes no difference. We must love them, and only when we truly love them shall we be able to bring them the witness of truth. That is what we are here for.

Worship meeting, Rhön Bruderhof, July 17, 1933

We have learned by experience that human relationships are of two kinds and that both kinds have a powerful effect on us. The one is friendship; we feel close to those in whom we sense feelings akin to our deepest and holiest impulses and calling. The other is hostility; it stirs us just as deeply. Opponents of our way of life as well as personal enemies shake us up and challenge all that is holiest in our life.

Meeting with guests, Rhön Bruderhof, Sept. 9, 1935

It makes no difference who our enemies are; God loves each one of them, and we have no right to pass a final judgment on them. True, we have to reject the evil we know they have done, but they remain enemies whom we sincerely love.

Meeting with guests, Alm Bruderhof, July 25, 1935

We should be thankful to our enemies! We have found out that Jesus Christ's command, "Love your enemies," is not overstated or exaggerated at all. We realize that the command of the Spirit, "Love!" holds good for friend and foe alike.

Whether we encounter friend or foe, it stirs our hearts to the depths. When we are filled by the Spirit of Christ, anything that moves our hearts can bring forth but one resonance, one echo: that of love!

Meeting with guests, Rhön Bruderhof, Sept. 9, 1935

We know that we are surrounded by enemies of the Christian faith. In such times the sacrament of forgiveness is needed more than ever, for the enemy's furious hatred challenges us to meet him with the opposite. Our enemies are the very ones we should love by having faith and understanding for them, knowing that in spite of their blindness they have a divine spark that needs to be fanned.

Love for our enemies has to be so real that it reaches their hearts. For that is what love does. When that happens, we will find the hidden spark from God in the heart of even the greatest sinner. In this sense we must also forgive our enemies, just as Jesus asked the Father to forgive the soldiers who hung Him on the Cross, saying, "Father, forgive them, for they do not know what they are doing." (Luke 23:34)

Worship meeting, Alm Bruderhof, July 19, 1935

THE SWORD OF THE SPIRIT IS NOT THE SWORD OF WRATH

The sword of the Holy Spirit given to the Church is totally different in every respect from the sword of governmental authority. (Eph. 6:17) God gave the temporal sword, the sword of His wrath, into the hands of unbelievers. (Rom. 13:4) The Church must make no use of it. The Church must be ruled by the one Spirit of Christ alone. God withdrew His Holy Spirit from the unbelievers because they would not obey Him. Instead, He gave them the sword of wrath, that is, temporal government with its military power. But Christ Himself is the King of the Spirit, whose servants cannot wield any sword but that of the Spirit.

Rhön Bruderhof, 1930

Still, we cannot go to a policeman or a soldier and say, "Lay down your weapons right now, and go the way of love and discipleship of Christ." We have no right to do that. We can do it only when the Spirit speaks a living word to our hearts: "The decisive moment has come for this man to be told." Then we will speak to him, and at the same moment God will tell him. What we tell him must agree with what God says in his heart at the same time. If we understand this, we will realize that we cannot enter into the deepest talk with just anyone at any time. Faith is not given to everybody, nor is it everyone's concern at any given moment. We have to wait for the hour God gives.

Rhön Bruderhof, Oct. 8, 1933

In the Reformation time it was the movement of our brothers [called Hutterian] who by the thousands protested from the bottom of their hearts against all bloodshed. It was a moment of very special significance because barbarity and bloodshed had reached atrocious proportions only equaled in modern times. This powerful movement of the Brothers was decidedly realistic. For they never believed that world peace, a universal springtime, was imminent. On the contrary, that the day of judgment was at hand. They expected that the Peasants' War would be a mighty warning from God to the government.

To be aware that the world will always use the sword is realistic. But that realism must be combined with the certainty that Jesus stands free of all bloodshed; He can never be an executioner.

He who is executed on the Cross can never execute anyone.

He whose body is pierced can never pierce or wreck bodies.

He never kills; He Himself is killed.

He never crucifies; He Himself is crucified.

The Brothers say that Jesus' love is the love of the executed One for His murderers, the One who Himself can never be a murderer or executioner.

Rhön Bruderhof, Feb. 14, 1935

DOES PACIFISM SUFFICE?

I really believe that much good is being said and done in the cause of peace and for the uniting of nations. But I don't think it is enough. If you feel urged to try to prevent or postpone a major European war, we can only rejoice. But what troubles us is whether you will have much success in opposing the war spirit that exists right now:

When over a thousand people have been killed unjustly without any trial in Hitler Germany, as of June 30, 1934, isn't that actually war?

When hundreds of thousands of people in concentration camps are robbed of their freedom and stripped of all human dignity, isn't that war?

When hundreds of thousands are sent to Siberia and freeze to death while at work felling trees, isn't that war?

When in China and Russia millions of people starve to death while in Argentina and other countries millions of tons of wheat are stockpiled, isn't that war?

When thousands of women prostitute their bodies and their lives are ruined for the sake of money, isn't that war?

When each year millions of babies are murdered by abortion, isn't that war?

When people are forced to work like slaves because they can hardly provide the milk and bread for their children, isn't that war?

When the wealthy live in villas surrounded by parks while in other districts there are families who don't even have a room to themselves, isn't that war?

When one person assumes the right to build up a huge bank account while another can scarcely earn enough for basic necessities, isn't that war?

When automobiles, driven at a speed agreeable to the owners, kill sixty thousand people a year in the United States, isn't that war?

Meeting with guests, Alm Bruderhof, Aug. 17, 1934

We cannot represent a pacifism that maintains there will be no more war from now on. This claim is not valid; there is war right up to the present day.

—We do not advocate the kind of pacifism that says the superior nations should have so much influence over the others that war would be eliminated.

—We do not support the armed forces of the League of Nations, which are supposed to keep the unruly nations in check.

—We do not agree with a pacifism whose representatives hold on to the root causes of war—property and capitalism—and fancy that peace can be brought about in the midst of social injustice.

—We do not agree with a pacifism that aims at a peace treaty while nations are actually fighting.

—We have no faith in the pacifism held by businessmen who beat down their competitors.

—Nor do we believe in pacifism if its representatives cannot even live in peace and love with their own wives.

—We do not believe in pacifism for the benefits it brings us or for the advantages to one's own nation or business.

Since there are so many kinds of pacifism we cannot believe in, we would rather not use the word pacifism at all. But we are friends of peace, and we want to help bring about peace. Jesus said, "Blessed are the peacemakers!" (Matt. 5:9) And if we really want peace, we must represent it in all areas of life. So we must do nothing that conflicts with love. That means we cannot kill anyone; we cannot harm anyone in business; we cannot lend our approval to a way of life that provides a lower standard of living for manual workers than for people in academic positions.

Meeting with guests, Rhön Bruderhof, Aug. 9, 1934

Nowhere does Jesus say a single word to support pacifism for the sake of its usefulness or benefits. In Jesus we find the deepest reason for living in total non-violence, for never injuring or harming our fellow human beings, body or soul. Where does this deep inner direction He gives us come from? It has its roots in the very deepest area that we sense in one another: the brother or sister in every human being, something of the inner light of truth, the inner light of God and His Spirit. (1 John 2:10)

There are some who misunderstand Jesus utterly and think there was a kind of unmanly softness in Him. His own words prove that this is not true; He says that His way will lead us into the hardest battles, not only into desperate inner conflicts but even into physical death. His own death and His whole conduct prove it—the sureness and fearlessness with which He met the powers of murder and lying. (Luke 22:42–44)

Members' meeting, Rhön Bruderhof, June 14, 1932

ENDURE WRONG, DON'T DO IT

Paul says: "Eat what is set before you without inquiring where it came from, even if it may have been connected with the odious customs of idolatry." The main thing is that you did not take part in the idolatry. (1 Cor. 10:25–31) This is a remarkable way of looking at the problem. . . .

It would be unthinkable for Jesus to carry on a hunger strike if He were in prison. That would be out of keeping with His way. If we are thrown into prison and the authorities provide us with our daily meals, we should accept them like children. But if the authorities expect us to do a job in the prison that directly or indirectly serves the military, we should refuse to do it.

So it is clear where we have to draw the line. I could also put it this way: Endure wrong, but do not do wrong. And if you have to suffer any injustice, your duty is to do your utmost to oppose it in the way Jesus did when He prayed, "Forgive them, for they know not what they do."

Rhön Bruderhof, Spring 1933

Death, we know, is life's most powerful enemy. Therefore we are against killing people. We know that it is relatively unimportant whether a person dies today or thirty years later, provided he or she is inwardly ready for Eternity. But death is something so tremendous and irreversible that we leave the power over life and death to God alone. (Rom. 12:19) We ourselves will not presume to shorten the life of a human being. We refuse to commit such a crime against life created by God. If we believe that death is the last enemy and that Christ overcame it, we cannot agree to serve death by killing people.

Rhön Bruderhof, 1933

Attitude to Government

THE GOVERNMENT HAS OUR RESPECT

We give our full consent to the government and its legitimate fight against sin and crime: lying, impurity, murder, and avarice. We are glad to cooperate with the authorities insofar as they try to do something constructive to counteract these horrible things. For we recognize the God-given supremacy of the government to the extent that it pursues the good and combats evil and does not overstep the limits set by God. (1 Pet. 2:13–17)

Meeting with guests, Rhön Bruderhof, Dec. 1932

What does Jesus tell us? Show your love to those who represent the government. You are not to take revenge but to meet the authorities with love. Then, too, pray for the government. (1 Tim. 2:1–2) It is utterly different from the Body of Christ, but it too serves God, though in a completely different sphere. The authorities are necessary; crime could not be kept under any kind of control without them. So you should recognize government authority but not become part of it. You are members of Christ, and Christ specifically rejected becoming a ruler. When they wanted to make Him a king, He escaped. (John 6:15) And when the Tempter came to Him and said, "Here, I will give you all the kingdoms of the world," He refused. (Matt. 4:8–10) But He treated the authorities with respect.

Rhön Bruderhof, Jan. 25, 1935

GOVERNMENT HAS TO COMPROMISE

No government can exist without using force. It is impossible to imagine a State that does not use police or military force. In short, there is no government that does not kill. Nor can one imagine a government that does not resort to diplomatic lies to disguise the real state of affairs. Talleyrand* is reported to have said, "Speech was given to conceal thoughts." There is no government that does not make concessions to prostitution and other debasements of human relationships. There is no government that does not compromise with capitalism, mammonism, and injustice.

When Jesus said, "Give to Caesar what is Caesar's," He was talking about money. (Luke 20:22–25) He called money something alien, something He had nothing to do with. Give this alien stuff to the Emperor; they belong together, mammon and Caesar. Let the money go where it belongs, but give to God what belongs to God. That is what these words mean. Your soul and your body belong not to Caesar but to God and the Church. Let your mammon go to the Emperor. Your life belongs to God! Jesus means us to recognize the State as a proven practical necessity. But there can be no Christian State. Force has to rule where love does not.

Meeting with guests, Alm Bruderhof, Aug. 19, 1934

---

*French statesman, 1754–1838.

Therefore we take no active part in politics or in the use of violence. We make no concessions, we refuse to get involved; but we are not indifferent. Every politician interests us, whoever he may be. And we wish everyone in politics could hear about us and realize that there is a life of justice and peace, where people have joy in one another. We wish that all policy-makers might be guided by these goals and not stray too far from the way of peace and justice.

Meeting with guests, Alm Bruderhof, July 2, 1935

If the government needs our help in a purely peaceful action, we are of course ready to cooperate. Only we must obey God more than men. (Acts 5:29)

Meeting with guests, Rhön Bruderhof, Nov. 1932

AN ORDER OF SOCIETY UTTERLY DIFFERENT

Hands off anything that causes hatred or unpeace! We must live like Jesus. He helped everyone, soul and body. We cannot go along with anything that harms people. As friends of peace we have to stay clear of any business practice or political activity that is not as Jesus would have it. The whole of our life must be dedicated to love. Our calling is not to use governmental force but to live the life of Jesus, who only loved and never had anyone put to death.

Meeting with guests, Rhön Bruderhof, Aug. 9, 1934

I have always maintained that today's world needs the law, government authority, and even the power of the sword.

Therefore they should not be abolished but seen as part of the effects of God's steps in history. Of course I feel, as I always have, that the life that flows from the heart of Jesus, from the innermost heart of God—the absolute truth—is completely different. It is a paradox, but you could say that the steps of God often go a different way from His heart.

Letter, Feb. 23, 1924

We do not withhold our respect from God-ordained government. (Rom. 13:1) Our calling, however, is a completely different one; it brings with it an order of society utterly different from anything that is possible in the State and the present social order. That is why we refuse to swear oaths before any court of law; we refuse to serve in any State as soldiers or policemen; we refuse to serve in any important government post—for all these are connected with law courts, the police, or the military.

Members' meeting, Rhön Bruderhof, Mar. 26, 1933

THE LAW COMES TO AN END IN CHRIST

Christ is the end of the Law. (Rom. 10:4) Faith has come. The taskmaster is done away with. However, human beings are still the same: As soon as they step outside the fellowship of the Spirit, they are once again subject to the law. If we step outside Christ and His fellowship, we are under the power of governmental authority. But God remains faithful; He separates governmental authority from the Church and separates the unity of the Church from governmental authority.

Rhön Bruderhof, 1931

It is interesting that the Confessing Church Synods gave the word, "No withdrawing from the Church!"* But that cripples every bit of initiative. For if the Church is godless, it is useless to say, "We protest, but we remain in the Church." If the Church is ruled by demons and idolatry, it is useless to say, "We protest, but we remain in the Church."

The reason for this limp attitude is clear. Even protesting groups in the Catholic and Protestant Churches render unconditional homage to the National Socialist State. They are willing to take active part in government functions. So what good is it if, from within the Churches, they protest about isolated incidents that lead to suppression of the freedom of speech, brutal murder, and all the other horrors, while they support the overall application of this evil system? The failure of the Churches of the Reformation to take the radical, early-Christian position in regard to State and society is taking its toll. We are paying for the historical sins of the Peasants' War: the bondage to the princes' rule and the outrages committed against the popular Anabaptist movement.** We are reminded of the way Christianity in England sold out to the State.

The cause of the error lies in a misunderstanding of Paul's words in Romans 13, "Let each person be subject to the governing authorities." Verses 1–5 have been quoted repeatedly by the established Churches to defend their interests in the State:

---

*The Confessing Church was a movement of resistance to the nazification of German Protestantism. It sought to resist the takeover of Protestant Churches by Nazi leadership without withdrawing from the State Churches. Its most important single expression was the Barmen Confession (May 1934).

**The first generation of the Protestant Reformation was deeply troubled by a series of violent uprisings of peasants in many German territories, 1524–1525. The reaction of Reformers Martin Luther and Ulrich Zwingli to this demand for social change was to commit their Reformation movements solidly to an alliance with existing governments.

Let every person be subject to the governing authorities.
For there is no authority except from God, and those that
exist have been instituted by God. Therefore he who resists the authorities resists what God has appointed, and
those who resist will incur judgment. For rulers are not a
terror to good conduct, but to bad. Would you have no
fear of him who is in authority? Then do what is good, and
you will receive his approval, for he is God's servant for
your good. But if you do wrong, be afraid, for he does not
bear the sword in vain; he is the servant of God to execute
his wrath on the wrongdoer. Therefore one must be subject, not only to avoid God's wrath but also for the sake of
conscience.

Verses 6 and 7 say that consequently Christians should pay
taxes.

For the same reason you also pay taxes, for the authorities
are ministers of God, attending to this very thing. Pay all
of them their dues, taxes to whom taxes are due, revenue
to whom revenue is due, respect to whom respect is due,
honor to whom honor is due.

But then comes Paul's answer to the role of government. First
the answer of love (verses 8–10):

Owe no one anything, except to love one another; for he
who loves his neighbor has fulfilled the law. The commandments, "You shall not commit adultery, You shall
not kill, You shall not steal, You shall not covet," and any
other commandment, are summed up in this sentence:
"You shall love your neighbor as yourself." Love does no
wrong to a neighbor; therefore love is the fulfilling of the
law.

And verses 11 and 12 speak of God's future:

> Besides this you know what hour it is, how it is full time
> now for you to wake from sleep. For salvation is nearer to
> us now than when we first believed; the night is far gone,
> the day is at hand. Let us then cast off the works of dark-
> ness and put on the armor of light. (RSV).

. . . We have been speaking about the divine origin of the
State, in a relative sense. (Romans 13) Now to speak about its
devilish origin, in a relative sense. Every connection with evil
is evil, and therefore it must lead away from God to the Devil.
God has instituted government authority only in relationship
to evil, that is, in a relative sense, and it must eventually fall
into the hands of the Devil. (Rev. 13, esp. v. 7) That is a difficult thought. This relative order is *not* God's will. Yet He does
not abandon humankind completely. He gives them a relative
order. If He were to abandon them completely, they would not
be able to draw another breath; as the Hutterian Brothers say,
"They would have no more puff in their lungs." They would
also have nothing more to eat.

God lets His sun shine and His rain fall on sinners and
good people alike. There is no human being who does not have
something that comes from God. (John 1:9) There is a divine
spark even in a prostitute in a brothel. That is why Dostoevsky's novels are so important. God has His order even in a
brothel, even in an army. But it is an order that belongs to
Hell. God maintains order, even in Hell. . . .

Government and police force are God's means of dealing
with what is evil in the world, not with what is good. We do
not deny the need for law and order in this world of evil. It is
an order instituted by God, but it is a relative order. But now
comes God's absolute order, which is love. (Rom. 13:8) In the
absoluteness of love there can be no active participation in

governmental power; in the absoluteness of God there can be no police force. We are dealing with two separate spheres: The one is that of evil and of the power of government; the other is that of love and of the power of the Holy Spirit. . . .

"You shall serve God alone!" says Christ. You shall serve Him in an absolute way, not in a relative way, as in the State. That is why Jesus refused to become a Roman emperor like Nero. He became Jesus Christ, and love was fulfilled in Him.

Meeting with guests, Alm Bruderhof, Aug. 12, 1934

World Poverty and Suffering

I AM GUILTY

When we speak of a radical social revolution, of turning everything upside down, of bringing in the reign of God's justice, we can only do so if we are deeply convinced that such an upheaval will affect us all quite personally, you and me, every single one of us, as part of humankind. We ourselves have to be thrown over and then put back on our feet. We are all responsible for the social injustice, the human degradation, the wrongs people inflict on each other, both public and private. Each one of us bears guilt toward all humankind because we are deaf and blind to their degradation and humiliation.

"Die Revolution Gottes," Die Wegwarte, *1926*

A whole web of guilt is spun round the earth, guilt that burdens our consciences. . . .

One of the petitions of the Lord's Prayer is: "Forgive us our trespasses," meaning our guilt. (Matt. 6:12) We have all had to see that we are involved in the guilt of the world. We are co-guilty if a whole village in Russia perishes of hunger, if war is waged in South America over a river. We feel we have a guilt in all these things. We feel it most in the question of unemployment. I feel guilty because so many children have nothing to eat. I share the guilt of the British government for tolerating the terrible conditions in India. I feel guilty because prostitution exists as real slavery, because money rules over people. We are guilty for every child who dies tonight! Our guilt is millionfold because of conditions as they now are on earth, and because of the appalling amount of sin. If we realize that, we will understand why Jesus said, "Forgive us our guilt" —not my guilt only, but our guilt!

Novice meeting, Rhön Bruderhof, Sept. 17, 1934

We are not isolated beings. We are parts of an integral whole, the human race. Humankind is harrowed by suffering common to all. A single cry of longing is wrung from it. Humankind waits for the day when all will be one. On that day the great catastrophe will bury everything that divides, and the new day of creation will dawn, bringing the joy of Paradise to take the place of all the world's suffering.

Public lecture, Berlin, Apr. 7, 1919

LAY DOWN YOUR OWN LIFE

We live in poverty and without personal possessions; we do this for love of Christ and for the sake of those who are poorer than we, the very poorest. There is such an endless amount of misery that wealth and affluence are unbearable to anyone living in the love of Christ. Undeniably, sin and injustice rule in the world today, and as long as this continues, there will always be poor people. It is idle to ask what we would do if there were no more poor. Even a rigidly enforced social system has not managed to do away with poverty. Therefore Jesus says, "The poor you have with you always."

And the Old Testament has it: "The poor will always be with you in the land." (Deut. 15:11) Yet this love for the poor cannot be the final thing. It must be surpassed by love to God. Christ says, "You will not always have me with you." (Matt. 26:11)

On the other hand, we must not let our love for God cause us to neglect love to the poor. Out of love to God we should love our neighbor. If you see your brother or sister in need and say, "God will help you," and give nothing though you have this world's goods, where is your love to God? (James 2:15–16)

Novice meeting, Rhön Bruderhof, Sept. 17, 1934

If someone wants to take away your jacket, give him your coat as well. Gather no treasures or showy belongings. Dress without adornment, make no attempt to be fashionable or elegant. Can you become a plain and simple person if you affect superior airs? If you become a true Christian, you will never have a fortune. Whatever you do will be done out of love. "Sell everything you have, and only then come and follow me." (Matt. 19:21) Do as the poor widow did. (Mark 12:42–44) Be true, and because you are true, be simple. Ultimate truth is ultimate simplicity. There can be unity in the Church only when all are true in absolute simplicity. . . .

After Jesus had told His disciples, "Gather no treasure for yourselves," He said, especially for the have-nots, "Do not worry. You must have absolute trust in God, who gives the flowers their beauty and the birds their food. Strive only for the Kingdom of God and His justice." Don't aim for a well-paid job. You will find the right solution in regard to your occupation. Strive only for the Kingdom of God and His justice, and include your wife and children in your striving. Then everything else will come right: the living of each hour and every day. That will make you a real disciple. You must not gather treasure for yourselves, and you must not worry. (Matt. 6:25–34)

Meeting with guests, Rhön Bruderhof, Dec. 1932

There is no greater love than to lay down one's life for one's brothers and sisters. (John 15:13) Laying down one's life does not only mean dying a heroic death; it means finding a life in which every moment is lived for others. In such a life we can give all our strength, all our fortune, all our possessions, and all our intellectual gifts for others.

That was the life Jesus lived. He did not ask whether Palestine was too small; He did not hanker after life in a palace in Rome. He acquired no titles or honors, He gained no influential position. He went the lowliest and simplest way. As a newborn child, He lay in a feeding trough for cattle. And His whole way was one of utmost poverty. It was the very simplest way, and it ended as it began—in utter poverty, in the poverty of the Cross.

Meeting with guests, Alm Bruderhof, Aug. 19, 1934

SUFFERING CAN DEEPEN FAITH

When we try to grasp the nature of suffering, we will feel that suffering is necessary in our search for fellowship with God. This is because of the inhibited and unredeemed life we live. We need suffering. The more we suffer and become aware of our own wretchedness, the more we realize that Jesus is our only foothold. Pascal never tired of saying that to realize our wretchedness leads to despair unless we acknowledge Christ.

Christ is our Redeemer; He knows the depth of our misery. He is our only access to freedom from sin and anguish. He knows our darkness and despair. He holds in readiness for us the strength and joy in life that can free us from our miserable plight. Jesus knows how laborious and burdensome our existence must seem to us, but He lives in communion with God's Spirit, who has the power to free us, and He has told us, "Your Father knows what you need." (Matt. 6:8)

Jesus knew suffering. He knew hunger and thirst. He had no place to lay His head. (Matt. 8:20) He had no house, no home. But He knew His Father, and in Him He had unbroken joy of spirit. Jesus proved to us that happiness in life depends on one thing only, on how well we know our Father in Heaven.

Public lecture, Dec. 1, 1918

When the day of judgment masses the clouds closer and closer together, we must be prepared to go the way of the Cross in utter surrender. Just as perfect love was once revealed in Jesus' condemnation and death, so the Church of Christ must complete what is still lacking in Christ's afflictions. (Col. 1:24)

We have to go still deeper into the willing acceptance of cross and death. Only when we are ready for this can we ask God to intervene and make His history.

Worship meeting, Rhön Bruderhof, 1933

The authority of the Church community lies in the charge given to it to represent God's Kingdom in the world. One consequence will be persecution. (John 15:18-20) We should realize without a doubt that we will be persecuted. The Hutterian Brothers have said repeatedly: We must be willing to be killed. We must be ready to have our homes, our land, our communal property, taken from us; these things are given us only to use in working for our fellows. Each one of us must be willing to give up life itself. And we will never be prepared to do that unless we are ready daily to do the hardest menial work and do it with joy.

Rhön Bruderhof, Summer 1933

Pain is the plow that tears up our hearts to make us open to truth. If it were not for suffering, we would never recognize our guilt, our godlessness, and the crying injustice of the human condition. (Ps. 119:67, 71)

Public lecture, Berlin, Apr. 7, 1919

It is not right to try to remove all suffering, nor is it right to endure it stoically. Suffering should be used, it should be turned to good account, for the glory of God. What makes a life happy or unhappy is not outward circumstances but solely our inner attitude to them. (1 Pet. 4:12–13) . . .

A precious stone has to be cut and polished if it is to be a perfected gem. Every good soldier of Jesus Christ has to suffer and wants to suffer. (2 Tim. 2:3) Steadfastness in the encounter with suffering shows that we are completely surrendered to God's will and yet have the courage to act. Both are needed if our lives are to be used.

Evangelisches Allianzblatt, *Sept. 19, 1915*

The deepest suffering of all is the isolation of the soul, the alienation of one person from another, the despair born of sin. In a divided soul, the conscience suffers anguish because it is separated from God.

Public lecture, Dec. 1, 1918

Yet deep suffering can bring us closer to God than anything else. In the helplessness of extreme suffering Job was driven to say: "Where shall I find strength to endure? I find no help in myself. My steadfastness is utterly gone." (Job 6:11–13) He was then led to trust in the strength that is greater than any other power. That was Job's purification. From then on he looked only to God, longed only for God, and was able to call out: I know that God, my Defender, my Redeemer, lives. Though my body be destroyed, freed from suffering I shall see God. (Job 19:25–27)

Public lecture, Berlin, Apr. 7, 1919

GOD CALLS THE POOR AND LOWLY

Jesus says, "I thank thee, Father, that thou hast hidden these things from the wise and understanding and revealed them to babes." (Matt. 11:25) Precisely those who are lowly and unworthy in the eyes of the world are called by God to do the most vital task on earth, that is, to gather His Church and proclaim His Gospel. (1 Cor. 1:26–29)

Again and again, what it amounts to is a clash between two opposing goals. One goal is to seek the person of high position, the great person, the spiritual person, the clever person, the fine person, the person who because of his natural talents represents a high peak, as it were, in the mountain range of humanity. The other goal is to seek the lowly people, the minorities, the handicapped and mentally retarded, the prisoners: the valleys of the lowly between the heights of the great. They are the degraded, the enslaved, the exploited, the weak and poor, the poorest of the poor. The first goal aims to exalt the individual, by virtue of his natural gifts, to a state approaching the divine. In the end he is made a god. The other goal seeks the wonder and mystery of God becoming man, God seeking the lowest place among men.

Two completely opposite directions. One is the self-glorifying upward thrust. The other is the downward movement to become human. One is the way of self-love and self-exaltation. The other is the way of God's love and love of one's neighbor. . . .

We pray for the whole human race to be released from the folly and delusion of exalting "wonderful" people. We pray that they may see that the meaning of history and of every human life lies in Jesus Christ, who is the new Man. He is the new Man toward whom we must strive in organic unity; then we belong to Him. Through Him and in Him humankind will be renewed. And this renewal will begin in the Body of Christ, which is the Church.

Worship meeting, Rhön Bruderhof, Oct. 2, 1934

This World's Revolution and God's Revolution

When someone asks us, "What is it like to live in community?" "How did you come to live in community, and how is your community organized?" we can only say that faith, quite specifically faith, is the seed from which community springs. We know that faith can move mountains. (Mark 11:23) That is the only help for humanity. Nothing else can help. Radical social revolution, idealistic back-to-nature movements, personality cults, pacifistic belief in the gradual improvement of the human race or in the power of good at work in history—none of these things can give humankind strength or show it the way. None of them can overcome sin, injustice, egoism, self-seeking, or greed. That is quite obvious, for example, from the words of members of the agrarian reform movement [for fairer use and distribution of land]. They say, "We take human selfishness for granted. Otherwise we could not stay in the reform movement."

Faith does not take human selfishness for granted; it counts on doing away with it completely. Egoism is then replaced by what Jesus tells us: that if we seek God's Kingdom and His righteousness as the first thing, everything else will fall into place. Then there will be but one answer to all questions: God's rulership in Christ through the Holy Spirit. I am convinced that no problem will remain unsolved if we follow this way in earnest and if this seed truly grows and thrives among us.

Meeting with guests, Rhön Bruderhof, July 1933

Bolshevism or political communism does not originate in spiritual fellowship or fellowship of faith and life, but in an ideal of centralized government and economy. It aims to force the communist way of life on the people. It approaches things from without. It tackles the outward problems of economic control. The hope is that the outward control will also help to improve inner relationships. Bolshevism can never create community by the use of force. Murder is not the way to peace. Killing is not the road to love. Bolshevism is a dangerous abyss; it is anti-Christian. Yet it can teach us that something better and purer must be given through Christ and His perfect love.

So the justice of God's Kingdom has to be something much better. Unless your justice is better than that of the moralists and theologians—and that of the Bolshevists—you cannot enter the Kingdom of God. (Matt. 5:20) The justice of Bolshevism is inadequate for the Kingdom of God. Its justice does not come from the heart, nor from spiritual fellowship. It is forced down people's throats. That is no way to build community.

Meeting with guests, Rhön Bruderhof, July 16, 1933

We have to find a different way. It is a very modest way because we refuse to attempt the reform of social conditions by political means. We abstain from all efforts to improve conditions by legislation; we refrain from playing any kind of role in the civic order of society. It may look as though we were withdrawing and isolating ourselves, as though we were turning our backs on society. In fact we are building up a life that is disengaged from the established Churches with their autonomy and self-sufficiency. We want to free ourselves of all these things as far as we are given the grace to do so and to follow Christ by living like the early Church in Jerusalem. Such a life means that a quite new reality has to determine everything in social, economic, and religious affairs, a new reality based on the unity and unanimity given by the Holy Spirit. (Ezek. 11:19–20)

Meeting with guests, Rhön Bruderhof, Mar. 26, 1933

That is the battle into which the communal Church is placed. The apostles refer again and again to the fact that we share in the martyrdom and Cross of Christ, for the zeitgeist will not tolerate the Spirit of Christ's future. (John 15:18–25) The zeitgeist does tolerate and enjoy our attempts at representing a little of the Spirit of the future and at the same time catering to people who are quite willing to make a few concessions. That kind of mixture is most desirable to the zeitgeist. Even the heathen State affects a mixture with the Christian spirit; the biggest capitalist enterprises want to have a bit of the Christian spirit, and deceitful undertakings of all sorts wish for a veneer of Christianity, a veneer of truth. Even those who go to war want to show some Christian love. This mixture is dear to them all.

Meeting with guests, Alm Bruderhof, Mar. 3, 1935

It is a paradox that the government, which is meant to suppress evil, by its very nature uses violence and thus is a beast from the abyss. (Rev. 11:7) If I may say something very bold, I would put it like this: God controls the hell of human crimes with an infernal machine, the State.

Now someone may say, "I am going to operate this machine and make it less hellish; I want to moderate the satanic properties of hell, so I will serve the State." Such a resolve commands respect. Very well; whoever wants to do that should go ahead, and I pray that such an undertaking may help a little. For myself, I refuse to mount the machines of hell. I will board the ship that shows all humankind the way to the other shore, which is not yet discovered. It is the Kingdom of peace, justice, and perfect love.

We need people who dare to set the course for this other shore, who dare to discover it, who dare to live in accordance with the ways of the land on the other side. But from this ship we intend to keep in touch with all other people. We have a message to send out to them, and through this we continue to carry our responsibility for the fate of humankind. We believe that this is the way we can best serve the world in this terrifying moment of history. (2 Cor. 5:20)

Rhön Bruderhof, Oct. 16, 1935

A brotherly revolution is one that calls for a uniting on all levels, inner and outer. Such a revolution is needed to bring about the desired freedom and equality in rich profusion and to lift all of life out of the sphere of human gain. But this upheaval, which lifts us all from the dust toward brotherhood, can never come from people but only from God Himself. God's will is loving unity and holy reverence. It alone can transform the will to power, with its destructiveness and deceit, into a new will filled with the power of love.

"Die Revolution Gottes," Die Wegwarte, *1926*

We have often been reminded of what Johann Christoph Blumhardt and his son said: God waits for places where He can break in. [See Introduction.] Each individual has to open his or her window to let in God's light, and the same is true of the nations. The Blumhardts said that for the most part people do not make way for God to act, but in their self-will and arrogance put their own actions in place of His. If only there is somewhere a place where people are completely united in waiting for God alone to act, He will intervene in the history of the nations and of humankind. . . .

The Church is called to move God—yes, God Himself—to act. This should not be understood to mean that God will not or cannot act unless we ask Him to. But God waits for us to be ready to believe in Him, for us to be ready in faith to expect His intervention. It is His unchangeable will to act among people, but only to the extent that they have faith, that they are ready to ask Him to act, to accept whatever He does wholeheartedly and to respond with their own daily lives. (Matt. 7:11)

Worship meeting, Rhön Bruderhof, Sept. 2, 1935

What we seek in calling upon God is an action that is not ours, a deed that is not our doing, a fact that we cannot create. What we seek in prayer is for something to occur that can never occur through us, for something to happen at last that we can never cause to happen. It is for something to be prepared that we can never prepare, for history to be made that we can never make, for a judgment to come to us that we can never summon.

The object of our prayer has to be what God has wanted all along. He is only waiting for us to be ready. This readiness is true prayer. God will come to us in answer to true prayer.

Alm Bruderhof, June 1, 1934

So the Holy Spirit comes to us in prayer, into our worship meetings. Not only does the individual forget his or her personal situation; the Brotherhood as a body transcends its own authority. The Spirit of the future comes to us and drives us into the future of the whole universe. For the Spirit whom we ask to come down to us wants to grip not only us but the whole world. That is why we ask Him to come and shatter the whole world at this very moment. We believe that our worship meetings are historic hours for the whole world.

And so we pray in our meetings to be united in faith that God will intervene in present history, that God will make history leading to His end-history.

That is what the first Christians prayed for in the name of Jesus Christ.

Worship meeting, 1935

The call to the tragic way of the Cross, to the revolution and judgment that has to precede the new creation, must be heard again in our day. We all hear it in the prophetic words of Jesus: "Change your lives to the very foundations, for the reign of God is at hand." (Matt. 4:17) . . .

The early-Christian revolution of faith rests on the certainty that each individual, all of society, yes, the whole atmosphere surrounding the earth, will be freed from the dominion of evil. The present economic and political powers will be overthrown, and God will establish His rule.

"Die Revolution Gottes," Die Wegwarte, *1926*

To be ready is everything! Let us be ready! The expectation of God's coming shall be our active readiness. That means stretching out our hands to Him in order to be crucified with Him. It means going down on our knees, ready to be humbled by Him. It means laying down all our power over ourselves so that He alone may have power over us.

In these days of wrath and judgment the heart of Christ is needed all the more to blaze up in the world and in history. The Church is sent into the world for this purpose: in the midst of the mounting waves of panic, in the midst of the furious breakers of spilt blood, the Church must fling itself against the waves and bring the banner of love to those who are drowning in loveless wrath.

For this we must be ready. Therefore, at the same moment while pleading for His day to dawn, we ask God to send us out. And not only to those few people whom we meet here on our hill, but to all, including the rich and the oppressed—especially the oppressed. But also as prophets to the wealthy, just as John the Baptist once went to Herod and sacrificed his head. (Mark 6:17–29)

We cannot ask for God to come, for Christ's way to be followed, for the Holy Spirit to send down His stream, unless we for our part are ready for the utmost. And we all have to be completely agreed about this. Only if we are one in what we ask God for will He grant it, but then He surely will.

Rhön Bruderhof, 1933

Postscript

We still affirm the witness of Eberhard Arnold. It is a direction for our lives. We are grateful for the miracle of over sixty years in community. It is also a miracle that obstacles to unity—touchiness, wanting to be right, and envy—keep being overcome. It is a miracle if the leadership problems of pride and ambition keep getting resolved, if internal conflicts are reconciled through direct speaking and forgiveness. It is also a miracle if the witness for peace and justice is maintained. And it is a miracle if we keep on being able to feed our children, maintain our houses, and find a market for our products. ("Community Playthings," a line of play equipment for children, and "Rifton Equipment for the Handicapped" are the main material products of our communities.)

It is providential when we can give each young person the education and training needed to make a living and stand alone. Everyone must come to his or her own way of life. It is pure grace each time one of our young people makes his or her decision to become a member of our community.

Our four communities have one common purse. We trust in divine protection and keep no money in the bank from one year to the next. We do not make plans far in advance, because we cannot know what tomorrow may bring.

On each New Year's Eve our late Elder Heini Arnold

(son of Eberhard) spoke out his wish for the year ahead as simply "mission." On one occasion he said,

> The older I get, the less important to me in actual fact is the Hutterian Society of Brothers. The main thing is that God's praying Church exists on this earth. And for this we want to give ourselves. For this we want to live. (*Worship meeting, Woodcrest Bruderhof, Dec. 11, 1977*)

We have tried to take that admonition seriously, constantly seeking to extend our work and our witness beyond our own gates, holding hands with others whenever we can. In the Civil Rights Movement of the 1950's and 1960's men and women stood up non-violently against injustice and tyranny. That great faith and courage, as well as the shaking deaths of Medgar Evers, Mickey Schwerner, James Chaney, and Andrew Goodman, and finally Martin Luther King, propelled us to participate in places like Selma and Marion (Alabama) with the Kings and others. Although we later felt we had to step back from the rhetorical violence of the Black Power Movement, something new was happening during those two decades, a rare stirring of the spirit. "We Shall Overcome" belongs in a special way to our black brothers and sisters who stood up, but they have always shared it with everyone who was prepared to stand with them. So—in the words of the song—we also asked ourselves during those years, "Do you believe—deep in your heart?" We still ask, and we cannot forget, and we still seek to be part of that search for a just and loving community.

During the Vietnam War years we marched for peace. Now the anti-nuclear movement calls for a protest of faith for the future. Recently we have been moved by obedience to the Gospel and by love for our fellow humans to visit those in prison. (Matt. 25:35–36) As usual, we have felt ourselves more on the receiving than the giving end.

One of our continuing sources of strength and renewal is the stream of visitors who come and are sent to us. For decades we have experienced mutual help and visits from the Christavashram in Kerala, South India (again through K. K. Chandy and his wife Mary in 1983). We have had several visits from the disaster areas in Lebanon. In 1983 the visits of Kefa Sempangi of Uganda, the John Perkins family of California, and the Vincent Harding family of Colorado expanded into mutually supporting bonds. As a result of our journeys and publishing in Germany three young journalists from Hamburg visited us. They were delighted to see "grandmothers behind computers" in our offices and challenged us to be "a city more on the hill."

That is our longing. . . . We also seek to reach out and learn and touch men and women in the troubled areas of this world. Thus we sent two of our community members to Nicaragua in the beginning of 1983. We continue to live in hope. We continue to be inspired by the words and example of Eberhard Arnold. We continue to be guided by the New Testament and its Lord.

> If then our common life in Christ yields anything to stir the heart, any loving consolation, any sharing of the Spirit, any warmth of affection or compassion, fill up my cup of happiness by thinking and feeling alike, with the same love for one another, the same turn of mind, and a common care for unity. (Phil. 2:1, NEB)

Woodcrest Bruderhof   *The Editors*
July 26, 1983

Addresses of the current Bruderhofs
of the Hutterian Society of Brothers:

Woodcrest, Rifton, NY 12471
New Meadow Run, Farmington, PA 15437
Deer Spring, Norfolk, CT 06058
Darvell, Robertsbridge, E. Sussex, TN32 5DR, England

Bibliography

Anabaptism and Hutterian Brethren

Dyck, Cornelius J. (ed.) *Introduction to Mennonite History*. Scottdale: Herald Press [n. d.].

Friedmann, Robert. *The Theology of Anabaptism: An Interpretation*. Scottdale: Herald Press, 1973.

Gross, Leonard. *The Golden Years of the Hutterites, 1565–1578*. Scottdale, PA; Kitchener, Ontario: Herald Press, 1980.

Hostetler, John A. *Hutterite Society*. Baltimore and London: Johns Hopkins University Press, 1974.

Peters, Victor. *All Things Common: The Hutterian Way of Life*. Minneapolis: University of Minnesota Press, 1965.

Eberhard Arnold and Bruderhof Source Material

(PLOUGH PUBLISHING HOUSE, RIFTON, NY)

Arnold, Eberhard. *Love and Marriage in the Spirit*. 1965.

———— (ed.). *The Early Christians after the Death of the Apostles*. Selected and Edited from All the Sources of the First Centuries. 1972.

————. *Sendbrief from the Alm Bruderhof to the Rhön Bruderhof.* 1974.

————. *The Meaning and Power of Prayer Life.* Vol. II of *Living Churches: The Essence of Their Life.* 1975.

————. *Inner Land: A Guide into the Heart and Soul of the Bible.* 1976.

————. *Foundation and Orders of Sannerz and the Rhön Bruderhof 1920–1929.* 1976.

————. *Children's Education in Community: The Basis of Bruderhof Education.* 1976.

————. *Salt and Light: Talks and Writings on the Sermon on the Mount.* 1977.

————, and Arnold, Emmy. *Seeking for the Kingdom of God: Origins of the Bruderhof Communities.* Selected and Edited from Earlier Sources and Memories by Heini and Annemarie Arnold. 1974.

Arnold, Emmy. *Torches Together: The Beginning and Early Years of the Bruderhof Communities.* 1971.

————, and Arnold, Annemarie. *From Hitler Germany to Paraguay 1937–1941.* 1982.

Hüssy, Gertrud. *A Joyful Pilgrimage: Emmy Arnold 1884–1980.* 1980.

Lejeune, R. *Christoph Blumhardt and His Message.* 1963.

Meier, Hans. *The Dissolution of the Rhön Bruderhof in Retrospect.* 1979.

Woodcrest Service Committee. *Eberhard Arnold: A Testimony of Church Community from His Life and Writings.* 1973.

Concerning other matters of documentation underlying the introductory narrative or the sources of the Eberhard Arnold materials, please send questions by mail to the Archives, Hutterian Society of Brothers, Rifton, NY 12471.

Name and Subject Index

Abortion, 180; contraception, 150–151

Acts of the Apostles, 43–44

Agape, 153

Anabaptism, 11–12, 19, 20, 188

Apathy, 123

Apostles, 49, 51, 120

Arnold, Eberhard: and baptism, 11–13; community beginnings, 18; conversion, 9–11; death, 5; and education, 20; family background, 9–10; and Hutterian Brothers, 19–20; legacy, 5–8; and National Socialism, 5, 21; publisher, 17–18; and Religious-Social Movement, 14–15; social concern, 10–11; and Student Christian Movement, 16–18; and war, 13–14; writer and lecturer, 13

Asceticism, 92

Atmosphere, spiritual, 104

Augustine of Hippo, 132

Authority, 115; apostolic, 81; Church, 128–129; civil, 175; God's, 40; governmental, 178, 186, 187; for mission, 53, 102

Baptism: see "Repentance and Baptism," 78–89.

Barmen Confession, 188n

Barth, Karl, 15, 17

Believers: see Disciples and "The Body of Believers," 111–117.

Benedictines, St. Benedict, 2

Bible, Scriptures, 42, 52, 63, 70, 143

Blumhardt, Christoph Friedrich, 15

Blumhardt, Johann Christoph, 14–15, 204

Brotherhood, 52, 115, 117, 119, 203, 205

Bruderhof: education, 20, 156, 160, 161; and God's will, 69, 75; guidelines, 49, 117, 142–143, 145–146; history, 5, 18, 19–21; objections, 102

Call, calling, 101, 106, 135, 186; Church's, 52–53; to mission, 104; of the Spirit, 173, 174; a way of life, 56, 69, 76, 99

Celibacy, 152–153

Change, inner, 51, 82, 86, 113, 127, 129

Index of Biblical References*

*References marked are quoted but not identified in text.